FOR OFFICIAL USE

Presenting Centre No.	Subject No. 1260	Level	Paper No.	Group No.	Marker's No.

	KU	EV

Total Marks

1260/103

SCOTTISH
CERTIFICATE OF
EDUCATION
1997

TUESDAY, 13 MAY
10.50 AM – 12.05 PM

CANCELLED

GEOGRAPHY
STANDARD GRADE
General Level

Fill in these boxes and read what is printed below.

Full name of school or college

Town

First name and initials

Surname

Date of birth
Day Month Year

Candidate number

Number of seat

1 Read the whole of each question carefully before you answer it.

2 Write in the spaces provided.

3 Where boxes like this ☐ are provided, put a tick ✓ in the box beside the answer you think is correct.

4 Try all the questions.

5 Do not give up the first time you get stuck: you may be able to answer later questions.

6 Extra paper may be obtained from the invigilator, if required.

7 Before leaving the examination room you must give this book to the invigilator. If you do not, you may lose all the marks for this paper.

SCOTTISH
QUALIFICATIONS
AUTHORITY

©

THB 1260/103 6/3/31960

1:50 000 Scale
Landranger Series

Four colours should appear above: if not then please return to the invigilator.

Extract No 1054/154

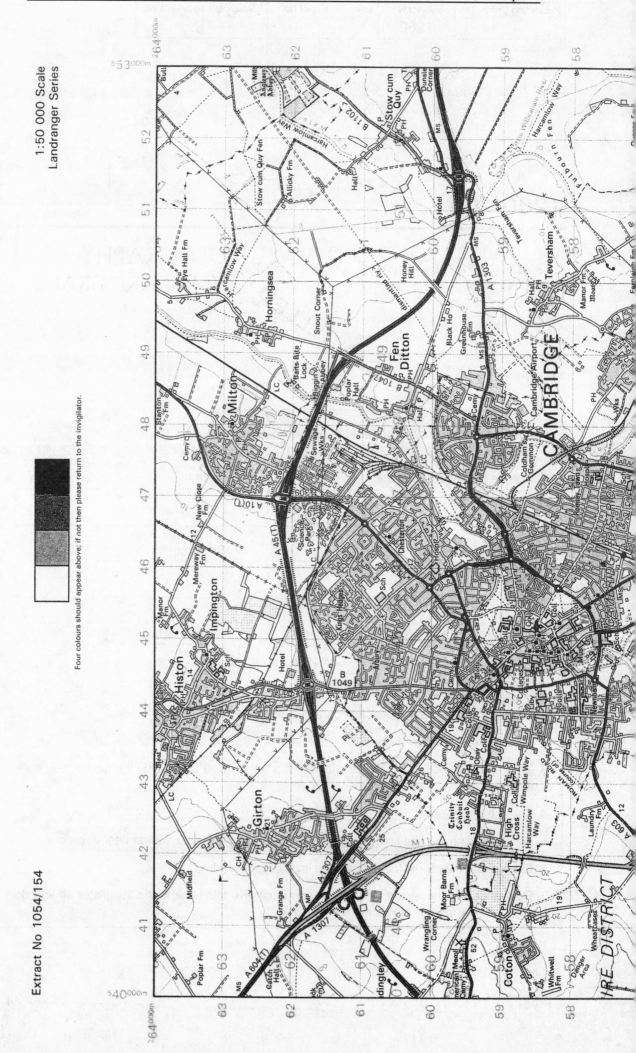

Scale 1:50 000

2 centimetres to 1 kilometre (one grid square)

Kilometres

Miles

1 kilometre = 0.6214 mile   1 mile = 1.6093 kilometres

Printed by Ordnance Survey 1996

© Crown copyright 1994

Reproduction in whole or in part by any means is prohibited
without the prior permission of Ordnance Survey.

Map reproduced from Ordnance Survey mapping with the permission of the
Controller of Her Majesty's Stationery Office, © Crown copyright, Licence No. 100036009.

1. Question 1 refers to the Ordnance Survey Map Extract (No 1054/154) of the Cambridge area.

Reference Diagram Q1

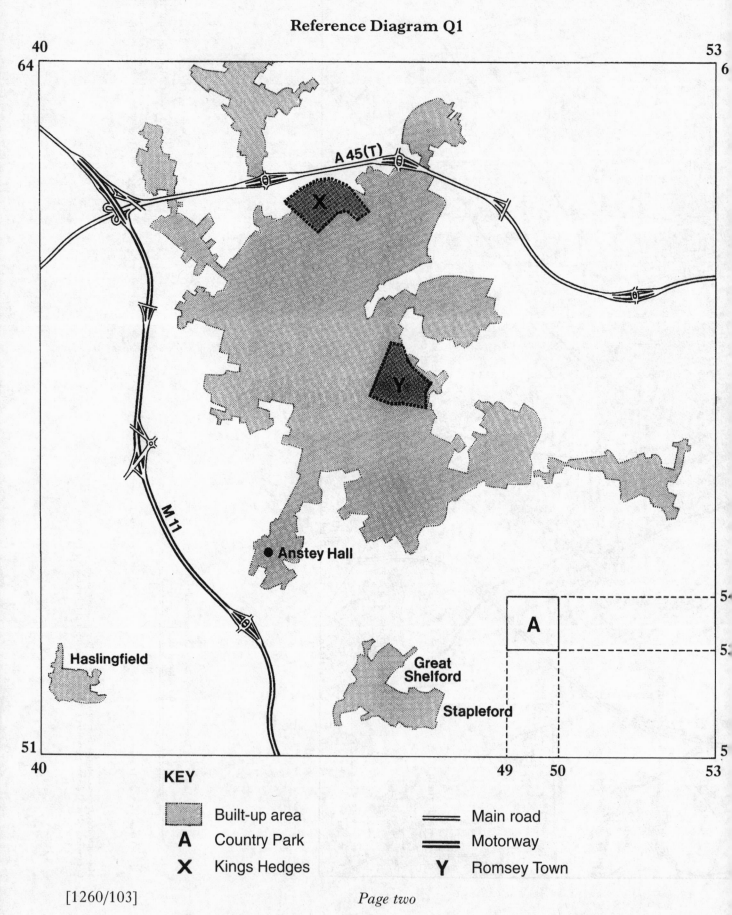

KEY

Built-up area   Main road

A Country Park   Motorway

X Kings Hedges   **Y** Romsey Town

KU EV

Marks

1. (continued)

(*a*)   Look at the Map Extract **and** Reference Diagram Q1.

Area **A** (4953) on Reference Diagram Q1 is a Country Park.

Describe the attractions which Area **A** offers as a Country Park.

_____

_____

_____

_____ **(3)**

(*b*)   Suggest reasons why Great Shelford/Stapleford (4652) has grown into a larger settlement than Haslingfield (4052).

_____

_____

_____

_____ **(3)**

(*c*)   Describe the differences between the two urban areas of Kings Hedges (**X**) and Romsey Town (**Y**) marked on Reference Diagram Q1.

_____

_____

_____

_____

_____

_____ **(4)**

[Turn over

1. (continued)   *Marks*

(*d*)   "It is unfortunate that planning permission for a new superstore in the grounds of Anstey Hall (443548) was refused. **This would have been a perfect site**."

Local Businessman

Using map evidence, **explain** why this statement is exaggerated.

_____

_____

_____

_____

_____

_____

_____

(4)

(*e*)   Identify **two** different problems the engineers faced when constructing the M11.

Using map evidence, show how these difficulties were solved.

Problem 1   _____

Solution   _____

_____

_____

Problem 2   _____

Solution   _____

_____

_____

(4)

Marks

	KU	EV

1. (continued)

(f) There are several colleges in central Cambridge. Many students use bicycles as the main form of transport.

Using map evidence, **explain** why this is a suitable form of transport in this area.

_____

_____

_____

_____

_____

_____ (3)

[Turn over

2.   Reference Diagram Q2: Glen Chanter estate in the Scottish Highlands

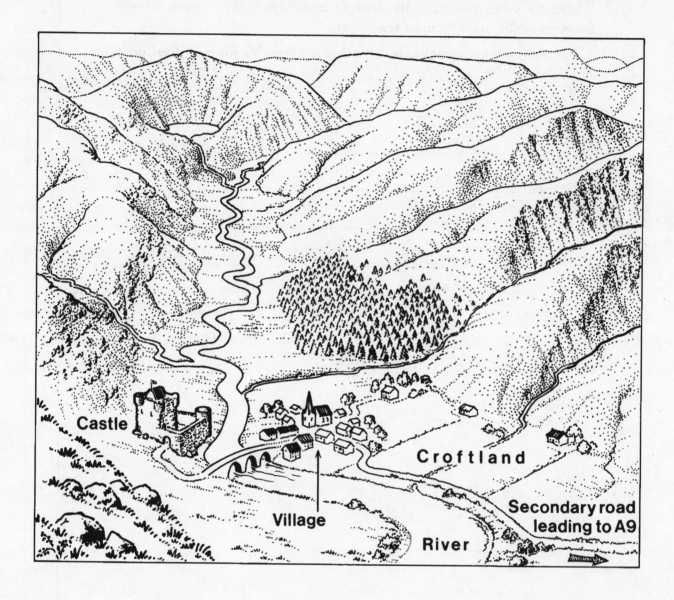

KU | EV

Marks

2. (continued)

Look at Reference Diagram Q2.

The new owner of Glen Chanter is considering four possible uses for his land.

The possible uses are

1. keep the land for deer stalking and grouse shooting

2. plant the area with trees

3. flood the valley for a reservoir and HEP station

4. make the area a Nature Reserve.

Choose **one** of the possible land uses and give arguments for **and** against it being the best use for the estate.

Choice _____

For _____

_____

_____

_____

_____

_____

Against _____

_____

_____

_____

_____

_____

_____ **(4)**

KU | EV

3. **Reference Diagram Q3: A Corrie in the Scottish Highlands viewed from the North**

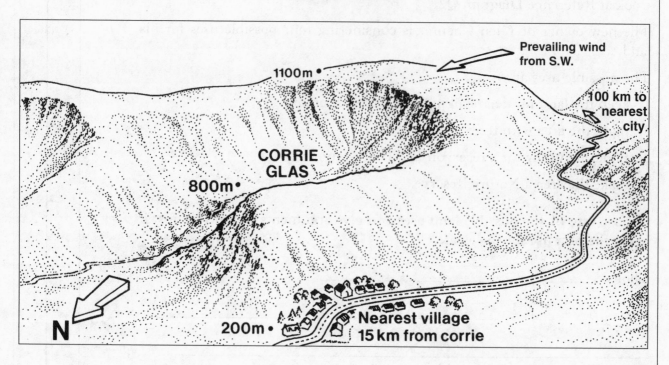

Marks

(a) Look at Reference Diagram Q3 above.

Do you think this north facing corrie is a suitable location for a new ski centre?

Tick (✓) your choice.   YES ☐   NO ☐

Give detailed reasons for your answer.

_____

_____

_____

_____

_____

_____

_____   (3)

KU | EV

Marks

3. (continued)

(b) **Explain** how a corrie such as Corrie Glas shown in Reference Diagram Q3 was formed. You may use sketches to illustrate your answer.

_____

_____

_____

_____

_____

(3)

[Turn over

4.   **Reference Diagram Q4A: Studying the Weather Forecast Sequence at Glenmore Lodge for Cairngorm Mountains on 24 April 1994**

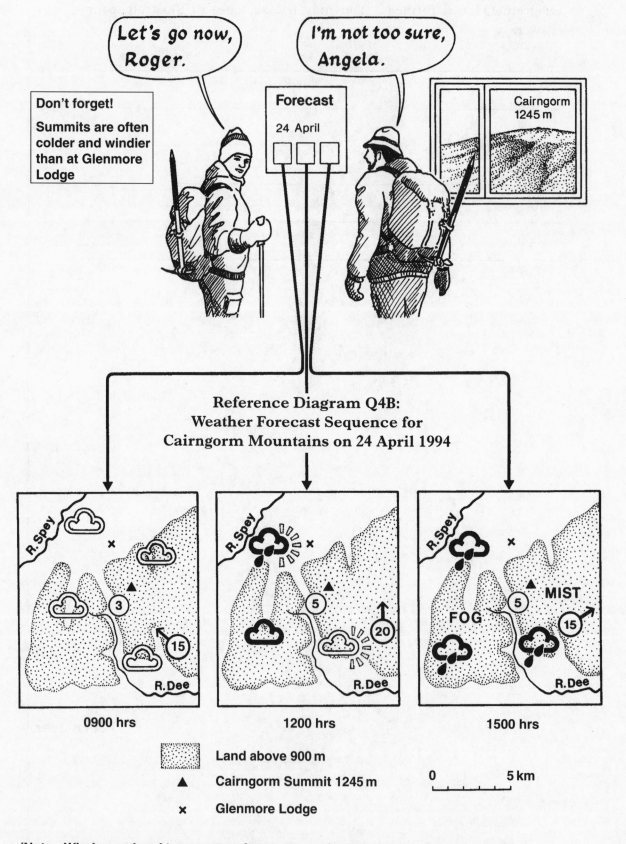

Reference Diagram Q4B:
Weather Forecast Sequence for
Cairngorm Mountains on 24 April 1994

0900 hrs   1200 hrs   1500 hrs

Land above 900 m

▲ Cairngorm Summit 1245 m   0   5 km

× Glenmore Lodge

(Note: Wind speed and temperature forecasts are for 900 metres above sea level)

KU	EV

4. (continued)

Look at Reference Diagrams Q4A and Q4B opposite.

Roger and Angela have travelled from the south to climb in the Cairngorms. They study the weather forecast before setting out.

Given these conditions, do you think they should go climbing on 24 April?

Tick (✓) your choice.   YES ☐   NO ☐

Give reasons for your answer.

_____

_____

_____

_____

_____

_____   **(4)**

[Turn over

Marks

5.   **Reference Diagram Q5: Part of the Rhine Valley in West Germany**

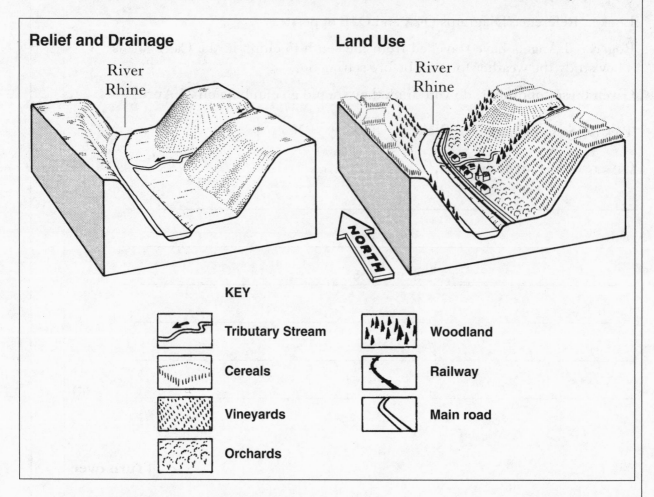

Relief and Drainage   **Land Use**

River Rhine   River Rhine

KEY

Tributary Stream   Woodland

Cereals   Railway

Vineyards   Main road

Orchards

Look at Reference Diagram Q5 above.

Describe how relief and drainage have affected land use.

_____

_____

_____

_____

_____

_____   **(3)**

KU EV

6.   **Reference Diagram Q6A:**   **Reference Diagram Q6B:**
      Land Use on a Farm   **Intensity of Land Use**

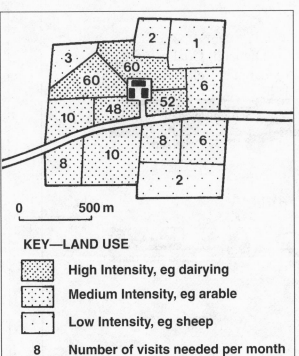

KEY—LAND USE

High Intensity, eg dairying

Medium Intensity, eg arable

Low Intensity, eg sheep

8   Number of visits needed per month

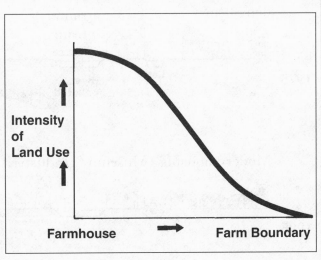

Marks

Look at Reference Diagrams Q6A and Q6B above.

(*a*) **Describe** the relationship between land use and distance from the farm buildings.

_____

_____

_____

_____   (3)

(*b*) What **human** factors, other than those described in 6(*a*), affect land use on a farm?

_____

_____

_____

_____   (3)

KU | EV

Marks

7.   **Reference Diagram Q7: Industrial Land Use—1975 and 1995**

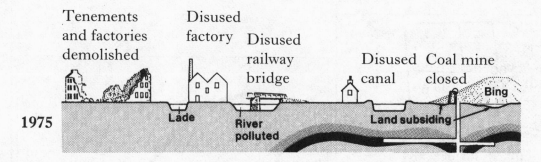

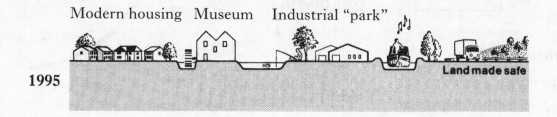

Look at Reference Diagram Q7 above.

(a)   **Describe** the ways in which the industrial landscape has changed between 1975 and 1995.

_____

_____

_____

_____

_____

_____

_____

(3)

(b)   For any **one** of the changes given in part (a), **explain** why this change has taken place.

_____

_____

_____

(2)

KU EV

8.   **Reference Diagram Q8: World Population Distribution**

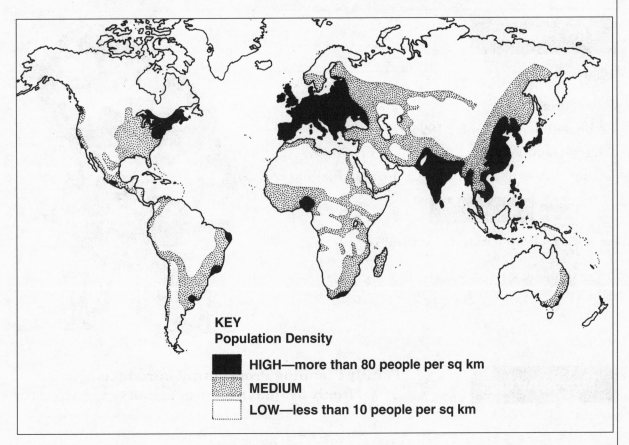

KEY
Population Density

■ HIGH—more than 80 people per sq km

▨ MEDIUM

□ LOW—less than 10 people per sq km

Marks

Look at Reference Diagram Q8.

Explain why some parts of the world are more densely populated than others. Refer to **both** physical **and** human factors in your answer.

_____

_____

_____

_____

_____

_____   **(4)**

[Turn over

9.   **Reference Diagram Q9: Family Planning in Thailand**

The Problem

1969

Population	26·4 million
Estimated population for 1994	67 million
Average family size	6·5 children
Living standards	Low and falling

 Thailand 1969

Population Growth 3% a year

GNP per head   US $ 110

The Solution

**Family Planning Programme introduced;
freely available contraception**

National Family Planning Programme

Ministry of Public Health

The Result

1994

Population	59·4 million
Average family size	2·2 children
Living standards	Still low but rising

 Thailand 1994

 Population Growth 1·4% a year

GNP per head   US $ 1,840

KU | EV

Marks

9. (continued)

Look at Reference Diagram Q9.

(*a*)   Give **two** reasons why a family planning programme was introduced in Thailand.

Reason 1   _____

_____

_____

Reason 2   _____

_____

_____   **(2)**

(*b*)   Do you think the solution attempted by the Thai government has been successful?

Tick (✓) your choice.   YES ☐   NO ☐

Give reasons for your answer.

_____

_____

_____

_____

_____

_____   **(3)**

[Turn over

10.   **Reference Diagram Q10: Comparison of USA and Japan (1990)**

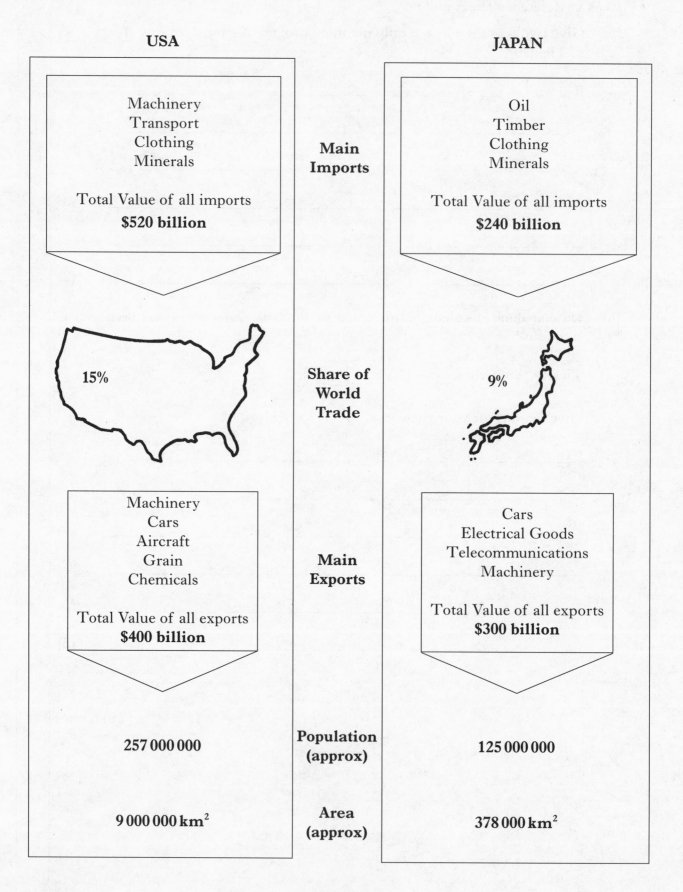

	USA		JAPAN
	Machinery Transport Clothing Minerals Total Value of all imports **$520 billion**	**Main Imports**	Oil Timber Clothing Minerals Total Value of all imports **$240 billion**
	15%	**Share of World Trade**	9%
	Machinery Cars Aircraft Grain Chemicals Total Value of all exports **$400 billion**	**Main Exports**	Cars Electrical Goods Telecommunications Machinery Total Value of all exports **$300 billion**
	257 000 000	**Population (approx)**	125 000 000
	9 000 000 km²	**Area (approx)**	378 000 km²

KU | EV

Marks

10. (continued)

Look at Reference Diagram Q10.

"Japan has replaced the USA as the world's leading economic power."

Do you agree with this statement?

Tick (✓) your choice.   YES ☐   NO ☐

Give **two** reasons for your choice.

Reason 1 _____

_____

_____

_____

Reason 2 _____

_____

_____

_____ **(4)**

[**Turn over for Question 11 on *Page twenty***

KU EV

Marks

11.   **Reference Diagram Q11: African countries where Uniglas does business**

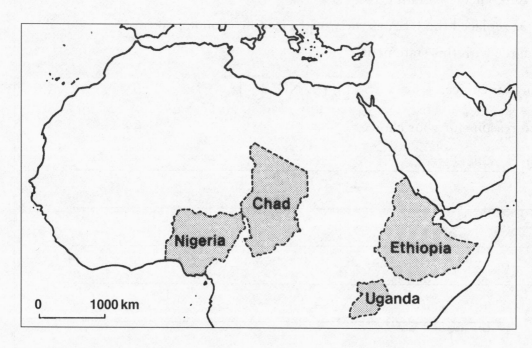

Uniglas is a **Multinational** Company which operates in many different countries and produces a wide variety of goods. It does business in the **Developing Countries** of Africa as shown on Reference Diagram Q11.

(*a*)   Give **one** advantage and **one** disadvantage for the company locating in Africa.

Advantage _____

_____

Disadvantage _____

_____   **(2)**

(*b*)   For any of the Developing Countries shown, give **one** advantage and **one** disadvantage of Uniglas operating in that country.

Advantage _____

_____

Disadvantage _____

_____   **(2)**

[*END OF QUESTION PAPER*]

KU	EV

Total Marks

1260/103

SCOTTISH
CERTIFICATE OF
EDUCATION
1998

TUESDAY, 12 MAY
G/C   9.00 AM – 10.15 AM
F/G   10.15 AM – 11.30 AM

**GEOGRAPHY
STANDARD GRADE**
General Level

Fill in these boxes and read what is printed below.

Full name of school or college

Town

First name and initials

Surname

Date of birth
Day   Month   Year

Candidate number

Number of seat

1 Read the whole of each question carefully before you answer it.

2 Write in the spaces provided.

3 Where boxes like this ☐ are provided, put a tick ✓ in the box beside the answer you think is correct.

4 Try all the questions.

5 Do not give up the first time you get stuck: you may be able to answer later questions.

6 Extra paper may be obtained from the invigilator, if required.

7 Before leaving the examination room you must give this book to the invigilator. If you do not, you may lose all the marks for this paper.

1:25 000 Scale
Pathfinder Series

Extract No 1100/SJ88/98

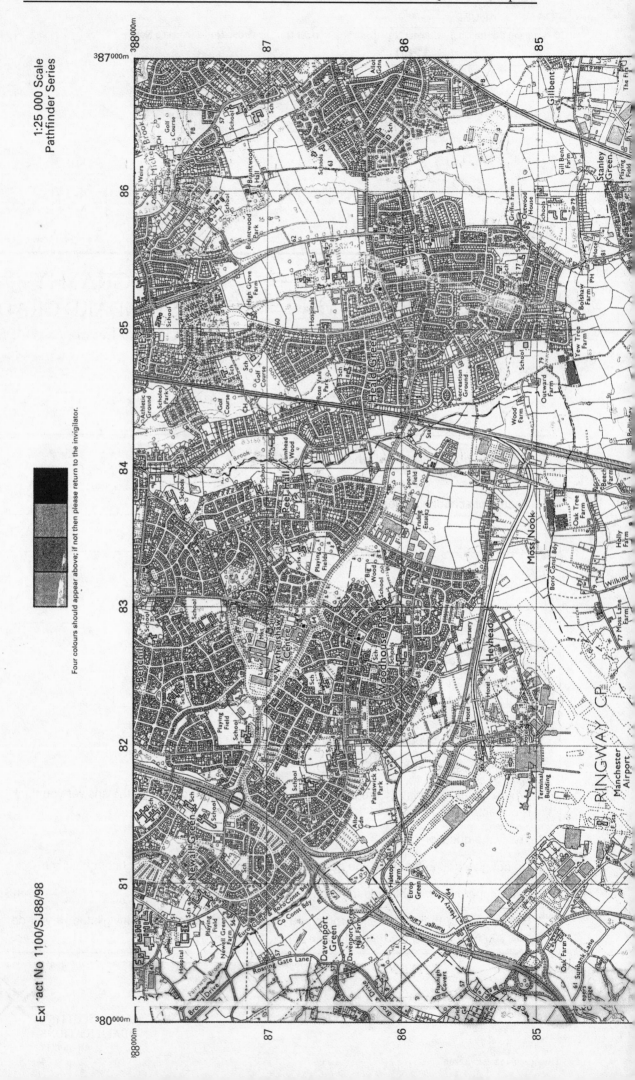

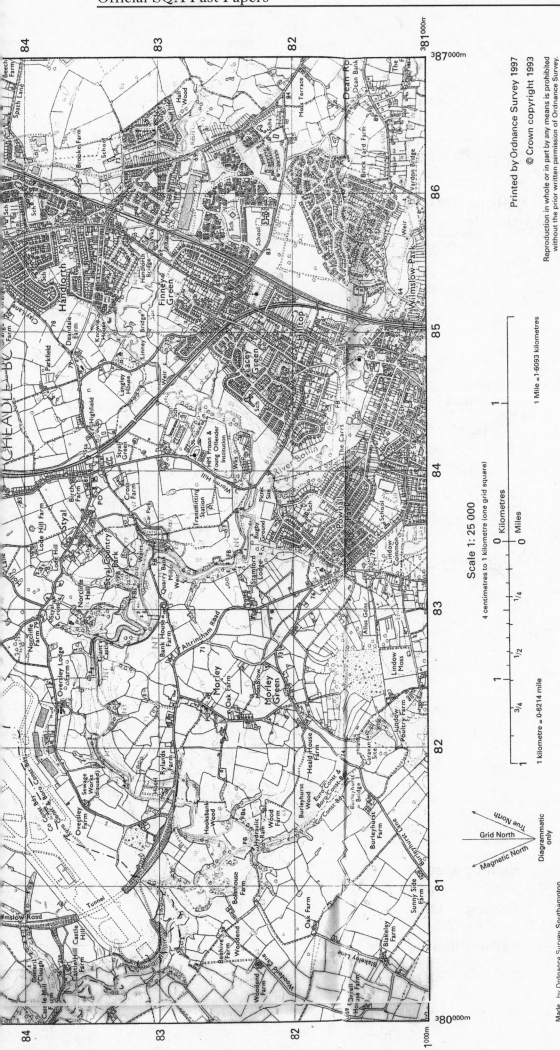

Scale 1: 25 000

4 centimetres to 1 kilometre (one grid square)

Printed by Ordnance Survey 1997

© Crown copyright 1993

Reproduction in whole or in part by any means is prohibited
without the prior written permission of Ordnance Survey.

Map reproduced from Ordnance Survey mapping with the permission of the
Controller of Her Majesty's Stationery Office, © Crown copyright, Licence No. 100036009.

Made by Ordnance Survey Southampton.

1.   Reference Diagram Q1A

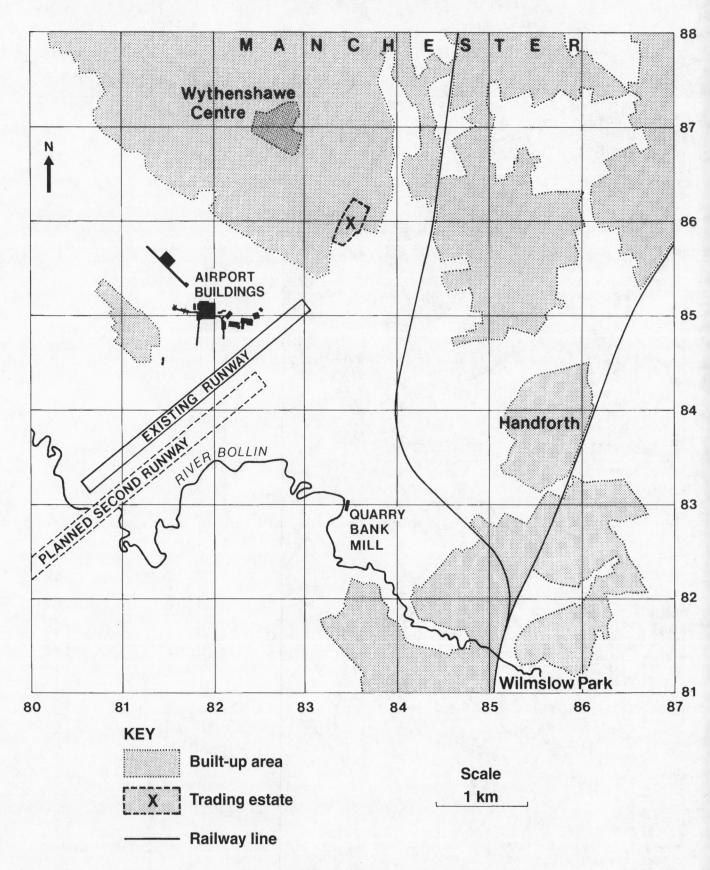

KU | EV

Marks

1. (continued)

Look at the Ordnance Survey Map Extract (No 1100/SJ88/98) of the south Manchester area **and** Reference Diagram Q1A on Page two.

(*a*)   **Describe** the **physical** features of the River Bollin **and** its valley from Quarry Bank Mill (834830) to where the river leaves the map at 800838.

_____

_____

_____

_____

_____

_____   **(4)**

(*b*)   "The main function of Handforth is to serve as a commuter settlement for Manchester."

Do you agree with this statement?

Tick (✓) your choice.   YES ☐   NO ☐

Give reasons for your choice.

_____

_____

_____

_____

_____   **(3)**

(*c*)   Using map evidence, identify **three** services provided by the Wythenshawe Centre (grid squares 8286 and 8287).

1. _____

2. _____

3. _____   **(3)**

KU EV

Marks

1. (continued)

Reference Diagram Q1B: Quarry Bank Mill

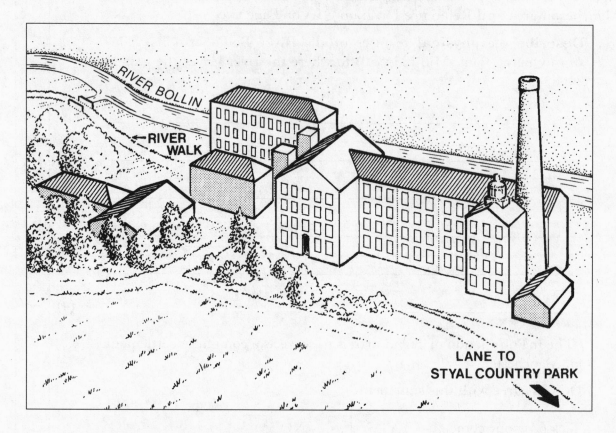

(d)   Study the location of Quarry Bank Mill (834830) on the map extract and refer to Reference Diagram Q1B.

Quarry Bank Mill is a former cotton mill which has been developed as a tourist attraction. Is this a good location for this tourist attraction?

Tick (✓) your choice.   YES ☐   NO ☐

Give reasons for your choice.

_____

_____

_____

_____

_____   **(3)**

KU | EV

Marks

1. (continued)

(*e*)   Area **X** on Reference Diagram Q1A is a **trading estate** (835860).
        Using map evidence, suggest **three** reasons why this site was chosen.

_____

_____

_____

_____

_____   **(3)**

[Turn over

1. (continued)

Reference Diagram Q1C: Noise levels around existing runway

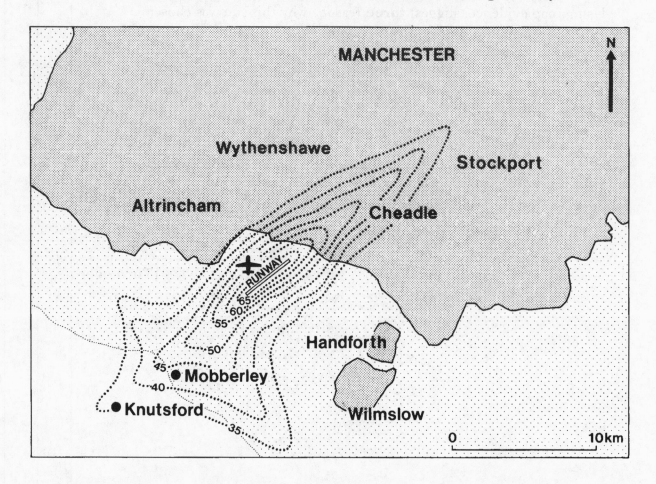

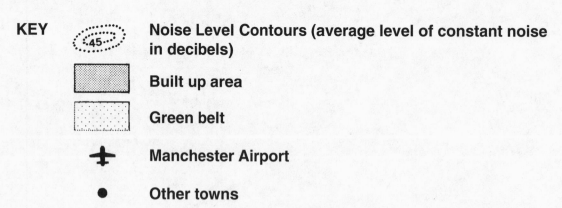

KEY

Noise Level Contours (average level of constant noise in decibels)

Built up area

Green belt

Manchester Airport

Other towns

Marks

	KU	EV

1. (continued)

(f) Study Reference Diagrams Q1A, Q1C and the map extract.

A plan to build a second runway at Manchester Airport was approved by the Government in 1997.

Give advantages **and** disadvantages of the plan for the area shown on the map.

Advantages _____

_____

_____

_____

_____

Disadvantages _____

_____

_____

_____

_____   **(4)**

[Turn over

2.　　　Reference Diagram Q2:　Weather Map for British Isles on 2 July 1995

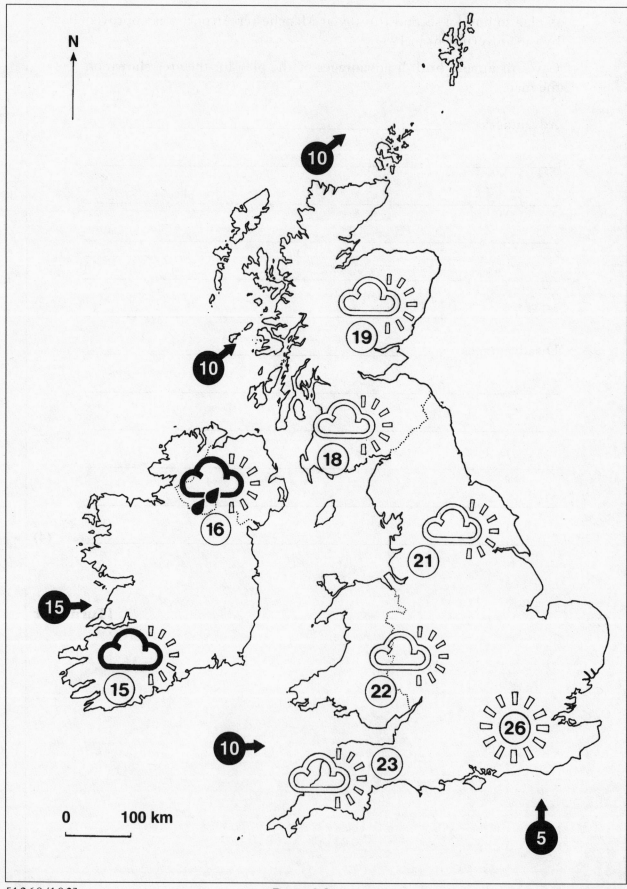

KU | EV

Marks

2. (continued)

Look at Reference Diagram Q2.

Describe the weather conditions in **Scotland** on 2 July 1995.

_____

_____

_____

_____

_____

_____   **(3)**

[Turn over

Marks

3.   **Reference Diagram Q3: Sketch of a Waterfall**

HARD ROCK

SOFT ROCK

Look at Reference Diagram Q3.

Explain how this waterfall was formed.

You may use diagrams to illustrate your answer.

_____

_____

_____

_____

_____

_____

_____

_____

_____

_____

_____

_____

(3)

KU EV

Marks

4.   **Reference Diagram Q4A: Climate Graph for Timbuktu, Mali**

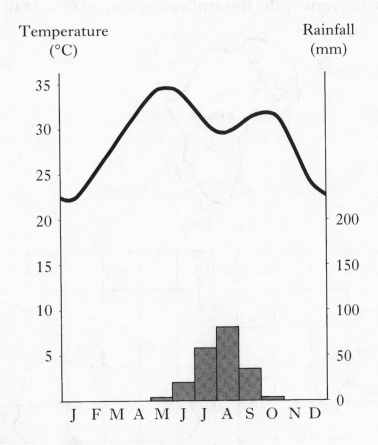

Temperature
(°C)

Rainfall
(mm)

(*a*)   Look at Reference Diagram Q4A.

Describe the climate of Timbuktu **in detail**.

_____

_____

_____

_____

_____   **(3)**

[Turn over

4. (continued)

Reference Diagram Q4B: Desertification around Gao, Mali

1975   **1985**

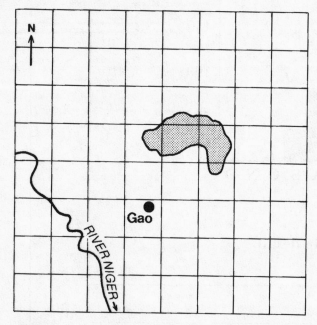
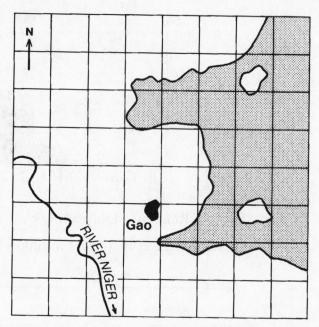

1996

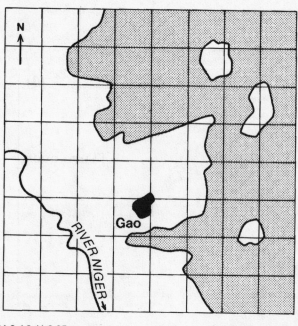

KEY

▦	**Area of desert**
☐	**Farmland**
●	**Settlement**

Scale

☐   **1 sq km**

	KU	EV

Marks

4. (continued)

(b) Look at Reference Diagram Q4B opposite.

Describe the changes in land covered by desert from 1975 to 1996.

_____

_____

_____

_____

_____ **(3)**

(c) Suggest reasons for the changes shown in Reference Diagram Q4B.

_____

_____

_____

_____

_____

_____

_____

_____ **(4)**

[Turn over

5.   **Reference Diagram Q5: Changes in UK Farming**

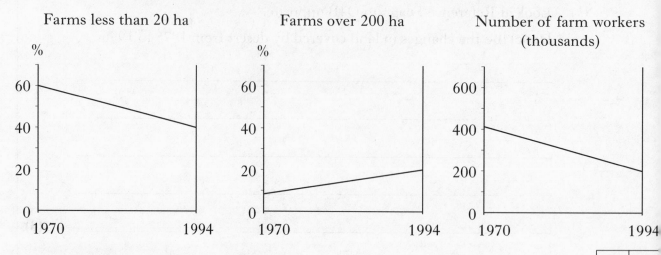

Farms less than 20 ha   Farms over 200 ha   Number of farm workers (thousands)

Look at Reference Diagram Q5 above.

Marks

(*a*)   **Describe** the changes in UK farming shown by the graphs.

_____

_____

_____

_____   **(3)**

(*b*)   **Explain** why these changes have taken place.

_____

_____

_____

_____

_____

_____   **(4)**

KU | EV

6. **Reference Diagram Q6A: Development of the Foinaven Oil Field**

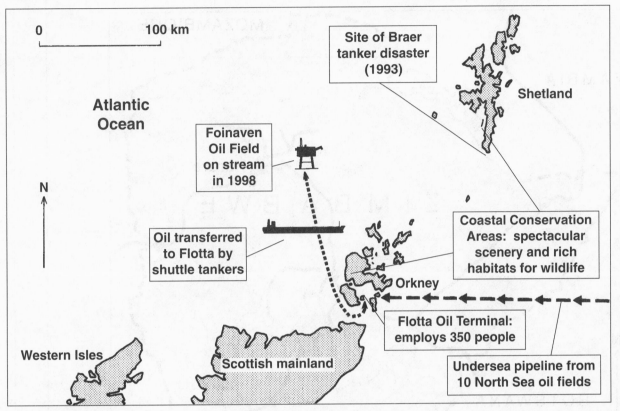

0 ____ 100 km

Atlantic Ocean

N

Site of Braer tanker disaster (1993)

Shetland

Foinaven Oil Field on stream in 1998

Oil transferred to Flotta by shuttle tankers

Coastal Conservation Areas: spectacular scenery and rich habitats for wildlife

Orkney

Flotta Oil Terminal: employs 350 people

Western Isles

Scottish mainland

Undersea pipeline from 10 North Sea oil fields

Marks

Reference Diagram Q6B: Statement by Oil Company Representative

"The arrival of oil from the Foinaven Field in 1998 is a tremendous economic boost which can only benefit the whole of Orkney."

Look at Reference Diagrams Q6A and Q6B above.

Do you agree with the statement by the oil company representative?

Tick (✓) your choice.   YES ☐   NO ☐

Give reasons for your choice.

_____

_____

_____

_____

_____

_____

_____ **(4)**

7.   **Reference Diagram Q7A: Cities and Towns of Zimbabwe**

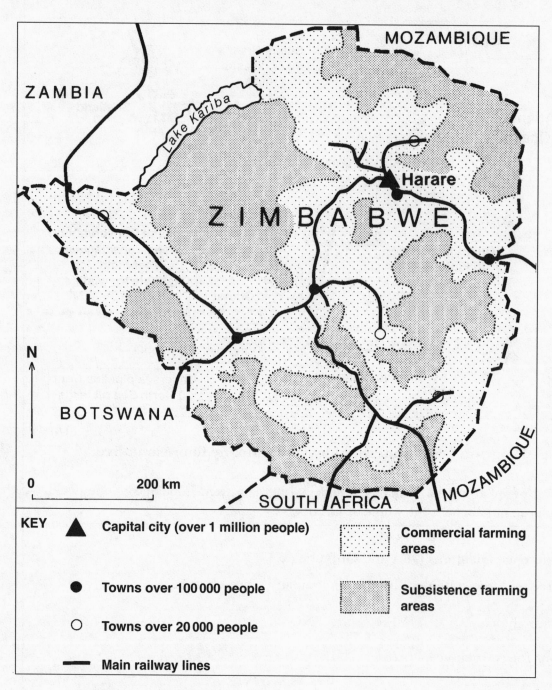

KEY

▲ Capital city (over 1 million people)

🔲 Commercial farming areas

● Towns over 100 000 people

🔲 Subsistence farming areas

○ Towns over 20 000 people

── Main railway lines

(a)   Look at Reference Diagram Q7A.

Describe the distribution of the main towns and cities in Zimbabwe.

_____

_____

_____

_____

_____

(3)

Marks

7. **(continued)**

Reference Diagram Q7B: Information on Harare

	1982	1992
Total population	658 364	1 134 169

(b)   Study Reference Diagrams Q7A and Q7B.

"Harare is the capital city of Zimbabwe, a developing country."

Give reasons to **explain** the growth in population of developing world cities such as Harare.

_____

_____

_____

_____

_____

_____   **(4)**

[Turn over

KU | EV

Marks

8.   **Reference Diagram Q8: British Aid to Developing Countries**

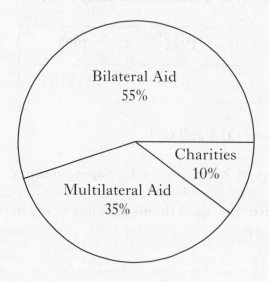

(a) Complete and label the graph below, using the information on Reference Diagram Q8.

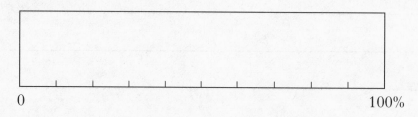

0   100%

(3)

(b) **Describe** in detail examples of the **three** types of aid shown in Reference Diagram Q8.

_____

_____

_____

_____

_____

_____

(4)

Marks

9. **Reference Diagram Q9: Tourist Development in Jamaica (A Developing Country)**

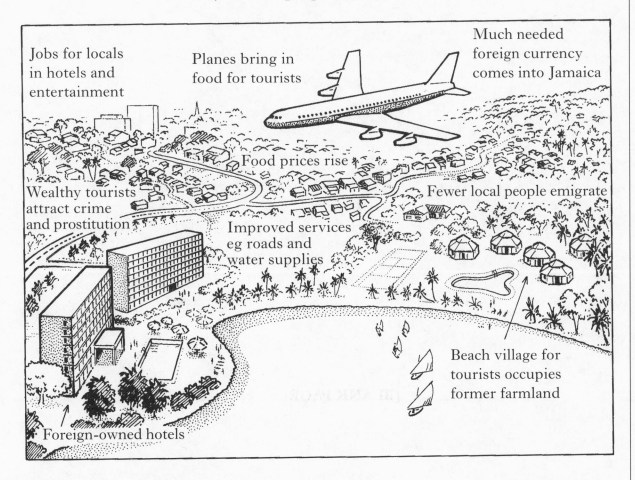

Jobs for locals in hotels and entertainment

Planes bring in food for tourists

Much needed foreign currency comes into Jamaica

Food prices rise

Wealthy tourists attract crime and prostitution

Fewer local people emigrate

Improved services eg roads and water supplies

Beach village for tourists occupies former farmland

Foreign-owned hotels

Look at Reference Diagram Q9.

"Tourism has solved all of Jamaica's problems."
—Jamaica Tourist Board statement

Explain the ways in which this statement is exaggerated.

_____

_____

_____

_____

_____

_____

(4)

[END OF QUESTION PAPER]

[BLANK PAGE]

FOR OFFICIAL USE

Presenting Centre No.	Subject No. 1260	Level	Paper No.	Group No.	Marker's No.

KU   ES

Total Marks

1260/103

SCOTTISH
CERTIFICATE OF
EDUCATION
1999

TUESDAY, 11 MAY
G/C   9.00 AM – 10.25 AM
F/G   10.25 AM – 11.50 AM

**GEOGRAPHY
STANDARD GRADE**
General Level

Fill in these boxes and read what is printed below.

Full name of school or college

Town

First name and initials

Surname

Date of birth
Day Month Year   Candidate number   Number of seat

1 Read the whole of each question carefully before you answer it.

2 Write in the spaces provided.

3 Where boxes like this ☐ are provided, put a tick ✓ in the box beside the answer you think is correct.

4 Try all the questions.

5 Do not give up the first time you get stuck: you may be able to answer later questions.

6 Extra paper may be obtained from the invigilator, if required.

7 Before leaving the examination room you must give this book to the invigilator. If you do not, you may lose all the marks for this paper.

SCOTTISH
QUALIFICATIONS
AUTHORITY

Extract No 1137/66

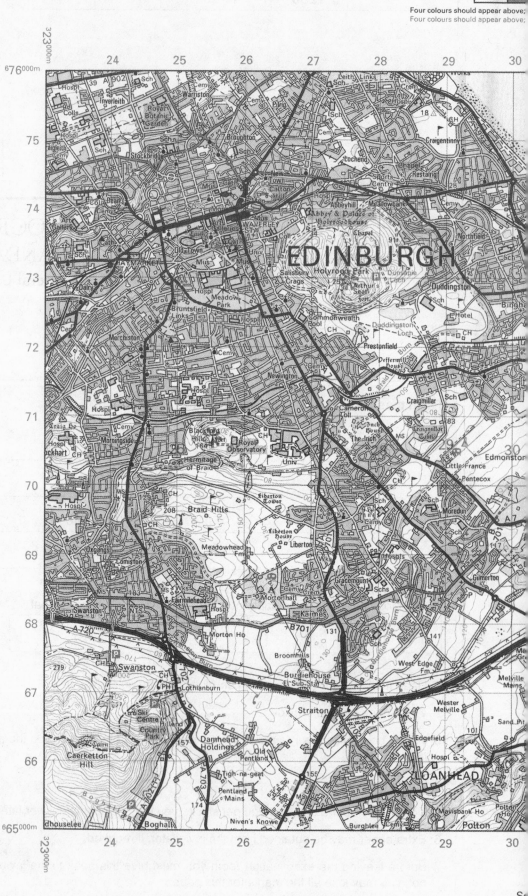

Magnetic North   Grid North   True North

Diagrammatic
only

2 centimetres

2   1   0

1   0

1 kilometre = 0·6214 mile

1:50 000 Scale
Landranger Series

1: 50 000

kilometre (one grid square)

ilometres   1   2   3

Miles   1   2

1 mile = 1· 6093 kilometres

1. Question 1 refers to the Ordnance Survey Map Extract (No 1137/66) of the
Edinburgh/Dalkeith area.

Reference Diagram Q1A

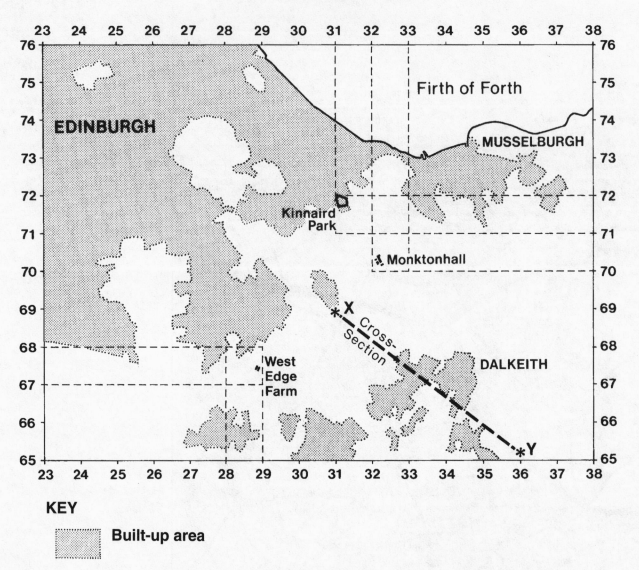

KEY

 Built-up area

KU | ES

Marks

1. (continued)

Reference Diagram Q1B: Cross-section XY from 310689 to 360652

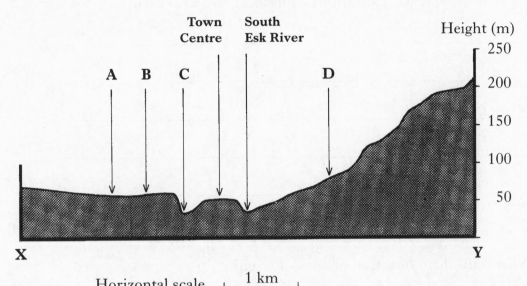

(a)   Look at Reference Diagram Q1B.

Match the Features (**A, B, C** and **D**) on the cross-section **XY** with the correct descriptions in the table below.

Feature	Letter
Woodland	
North Esk River	
A 720	
B 6482	

(3)

(b)   Using **specific** examples from the map, **describe** the ways in which Dalkeith's growth has been restricted.

_____

_____

_____

_____

_____

_____

_____

(4)

Marks

KU | ES

1. (continued)

    (*c*)   Kinnaird Park, a shopping and leisure complex, was built at 312718.

        Using map evidence, **explain** why this location was chosen.

_____

_____

_____

_____

_____

_____

(4)

    (*d*)   What is the main **function** of Musselburgh?

        Tick (✓) your choice.

        Holiday Resort ☐   Commuter Settlement ☐

        Use map evidence to support your choice.

_____

_____

_____

_____

_____

(4)

KU | ES

Marks

1. (continued)

(*e*) Match the following grid squares with the land uses shown in the table below.

Grid squares: 2573   2671   2372   2868

Land Use	Grid Square
Mixture of old housing and old industry	
Central Business District (CBD)	
Modern housing area	
Older housing area	

(3)

(*f*) West Edge Farm is located at 289674. Do you think this is a good location for a farm?

Tick (✓) your choice.   YES ☐   NO ☐

Using map evidence, give reasons to support your choice.

_____

_____

_____

_____

_____

_____

(4)

[Turn over

Marks

1. (continued)

Reference Diagram Q1C: Demolition of Mining Towers at Monktonhall

(g) Look at Reference Diagram Q1C.

The coal mine at 3270 was closed in June 1997.

Give the advantages **and** disadvantages of the closure of the mine **to** the surrounding area.

(You should refer to the sketch and/or map evidence to support your answer.)

Advantages _____

_____

_____

_____

Disadvantages _____

_____

_____

_____   **(4)**

KU ES

Marks

2.   **Reference Diagram Q2: Weather Chart for 1200 hours
on 25 November**

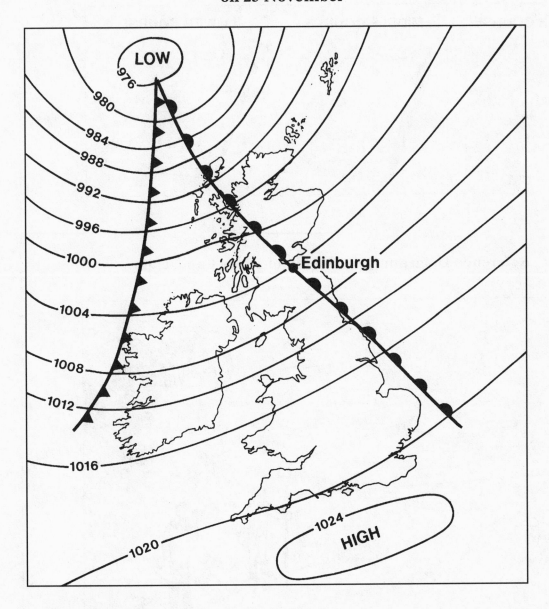

Look at Reference Diagram Q2.

Describe the weather conditions in Edinburgh at 1200 hours on 25 November.

_____

_____

_____

_____

_____   (4)

Marks

3.   **Reference Diagram Q3A: Three Stages of a River**

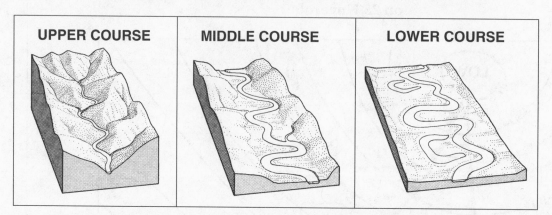

Reference Diagram Q3B: Sketch of River Landscape

KU | ES

Marks

3. (continued)

(a) Look at Reference Diagrams Q3A and Q3B.

"The valley shown in Reference Diagram Q3B is typical of the **lower** course of a river."

Do you agree with the statement?

Tick (✓) your choice.   YES ☐   NO ☐

Give reasons for your choice.

_____

_____

_____

_____

_____   **(4)**

(b) The pupils in Reference Diagram Q3B are about to do a river study.

What **two** techniques could they use to gather information about the characteristics of the river at **AB** on the sketch?

Technique 1 _____

_____

Technique 2 _____

_____

Justify your choices.

_____

_____

_____

_____   **(4)**

[Turn over

4.   Reference Diagram Q4A: Climate Graph of Tropical Rainforest

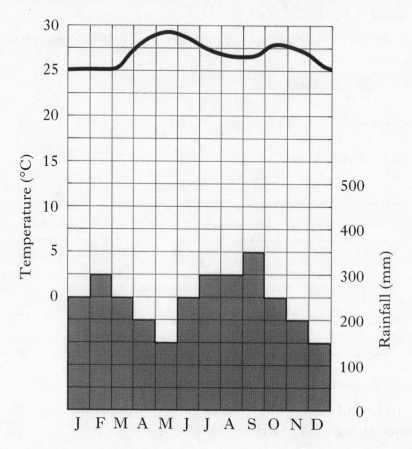

Reference Diagram Q4B: Developing the Tropical Rainforest

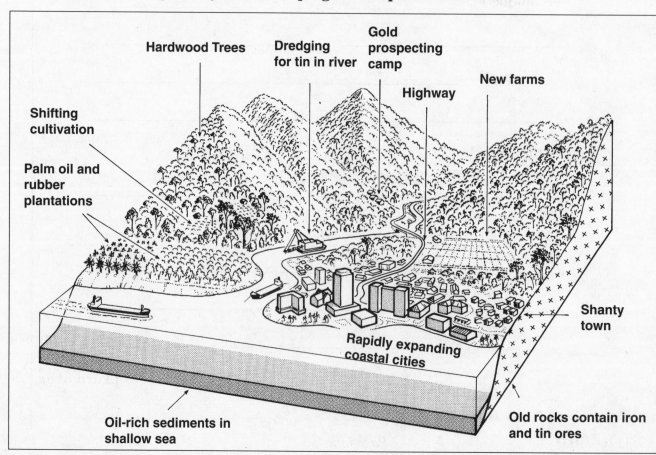

KU | ES

Marks

4. (continued)

(*a*)   Look at Reference Diagram Q4A.

Describe in detail the climate of the Tropical Rainforest.

_____

_____

_____

_____

_____ **(3)**

(*b*)   Look at Reference Diagram Q4B.

Describe the damage to the environment which could be caused by developing the natural resources of a Tropical Rainforest.

_____

_____

_____

_____

_____ **(4)**

[Turn over

Marks

5.   **Reference Diagram Q5: Farming Landscape**

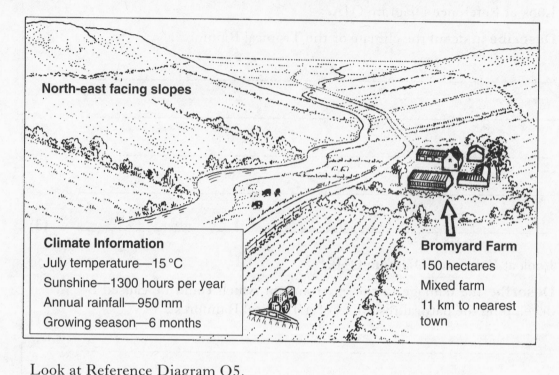

North-east facing slopes

Climate Information
July temperature—15 °C
Sunshine—1300 hours per year
Annual rainfall—950 mm
Growing season—6 months

Bromyard Farm
150 hectares
Mixed farm
11 km to nearest town

Look at Reference Diagram Q5.

"Mixed Farming is the most suitable type of farming for this area."

Do you agree with the statement?

Tick (✓) your choice.   YES ☐   NO ☐

Give detailed reasons for your choice.

_____

_____

_____

_____

_____

_____

_____

(4)

6.   **Reference Diagram Q6: The M62 Corridor**

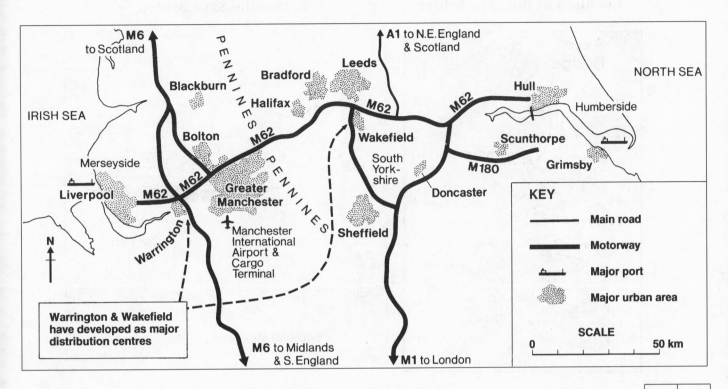

Look at Reference Diagram Q6.

The M62 motorway runs from Merseyside to Humberside. The area around it,
known as the M62 corridor, is often described as England's new economic super
region.

Give reasons to **explain** why so many companies are locating here.

Marks

(4)

[Turn over

7.   **Reference Diagram Q7A:**   **Reference Diagram Q7B:**
     Location of the Skye Bridge   **Before the Skye Bridge**

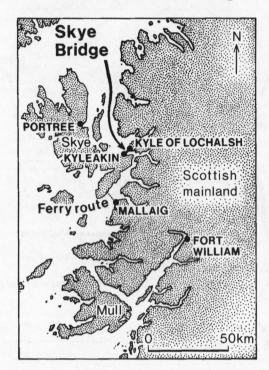

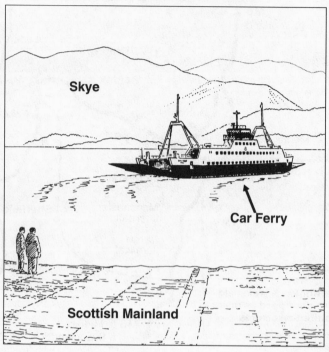

Reference Diagram Q7C: The Skye Bridge

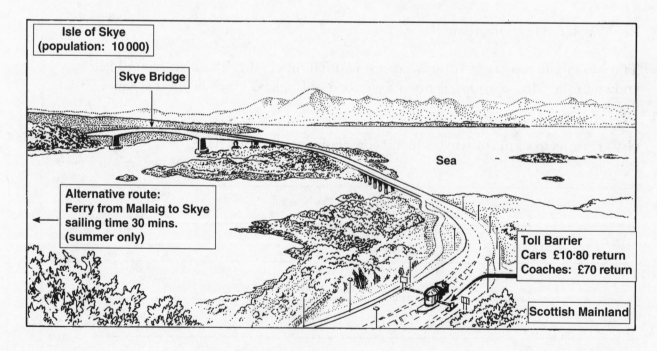

KU | ES

Marks

7. (continued)

Look at Reference Diagrams Q7A, Q7B and Q7C.

The Skye Bridge was opened in 1996 and replaced the ferry which ran from Kyle of Lochalsh to Kyleakin.

Give advantages **and** disadvantages of the Skye Bridge **for the people of Skye**.

Advantages _____

_____

_____

_____

Disadvantages _____

_____

_____

_____   **(4)**

[Turn over

8.   **Reference Diagram Q8A: Japan's Trade Links**

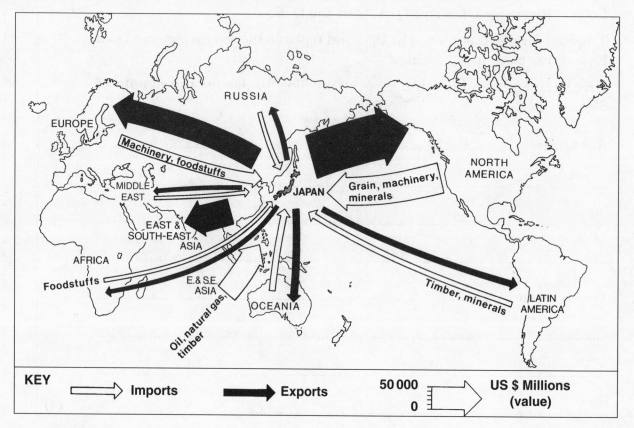

KEY   ⇨ Imports   ➡ Exports   50 000 / 0 ⇨ US $ Millions (value)

(a)   Look at Reference Diagram Q8A.

      Describe the pattern of Japan's trade.

      _____

      _____

      _____

      _____

      _____

      _____

KU ES

Marks

(3)

KU | ES

Marks

8. (continued)

Reference Diagram Q8B: Japan's Exports

Exports	Percentage
Manufactured goods	83
Chemicals and other raw materials	7
Others	10

(*b*)   Look at Reference Diagram Q8B.

Give **one** processing technique which could be used to present the information in Reference Diagram Q8B. Give reasons for your choice.

Technique _____

Reasons _____

_____

_____

_____

_____

_____

_____   (3)

[Turn over

9.   **Reference Diagram Q9: Distribution of Underweight Children**

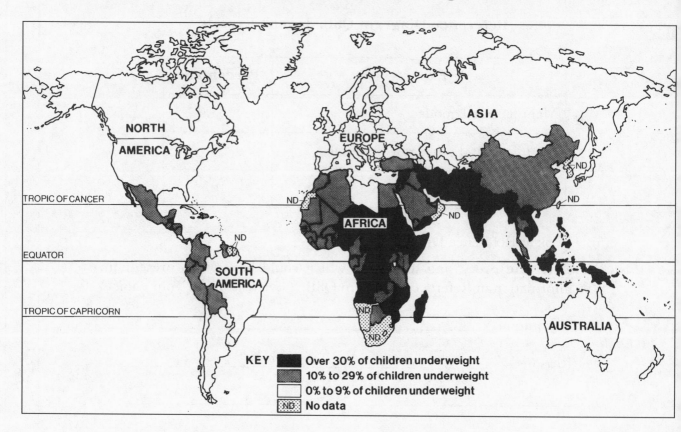

Look at Reference Diagram Q9.

(a)   **Describe** the distribution pattern of underweight children.

_____

_____

_____

_____

_____

_____

(3)

KU | ES

Marks

9. (continued)

(*b*) **Explain** why certain parts of the world have a high percentage of underweight children.

_____

_____

_____

_____

_____

_____   **(4)**

[Turn over for Question 10 on *Page twenty*

Marks

10.   **Reference Diagram Q10: Maps of Malaysian Peninsula**

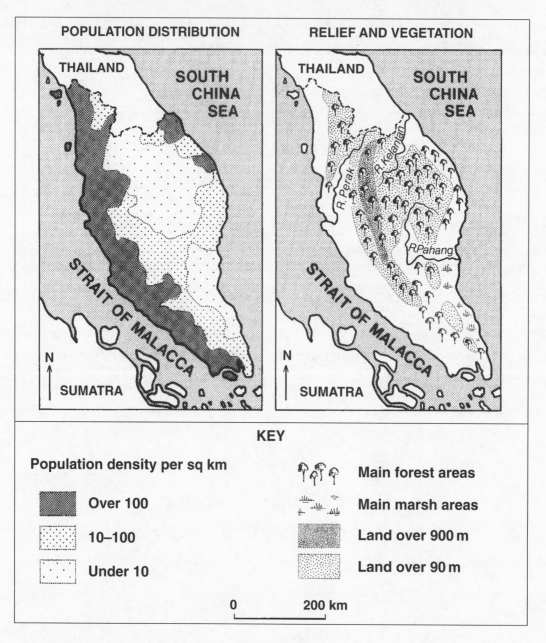

POPULATION DISTRIBUTION   RELIEF AND VEGETATION

KEY

Population density per sq km

Over 100

10–100

Under 10

Main forest areas

Main marsh areas

Land over 900 m

Land over 90 m

0   200 km

Look at Reference Diagram Q10 above.

Describe the relationship between population distribution and physical
features (relief and vegetation) in the Malaysian Peninsula.

_____

_____

_____

_____

_____

_____

(4)

[END OF QUESTION PAPER]

FOR OFFICIAL USE

KU   ES

Total Marks

1260/403

NATIONAL   MONDAY, 5 JUNE   **GEOGRAPHY**
QUALIFICATIONS   G/C   9.00 AM – 10.25 AM   **STANDARD GRADE**
2000   F/G   10.25 AM – 11.50 AM   General Level

Fill in these boxes and read what is printed below.

Full name of centre   Town

Forename(s)   Surname

Date of birth
Day Month Year   Scottish candidate number   Number of seat

1 Read the whole of each question carefully before you answer it.

2 Write in the spaces provided.

3 Where boxes like this ☐ are provided, put a tick ✓ in the box beside the answer you think
   is correct.

4 Try all the questions.

5 Do not give up the first time you get stuck: you may be able to answer later questions.

6 Extra paper may be obtained from the invigilator, if required.

7 Before leaving the examination room you must give this book to the invigilator. If you do
   not, you may lose all the marks for this paper.

SCOTTISH
QUALIFICATIONS
AUTHORITY

Extract No 1174/41

1:50 000 Scale
Landranger Series

Four colours should appear above; if not then please return to the invigilator.
Four colours should appear above; if not then please return to the invigilator.

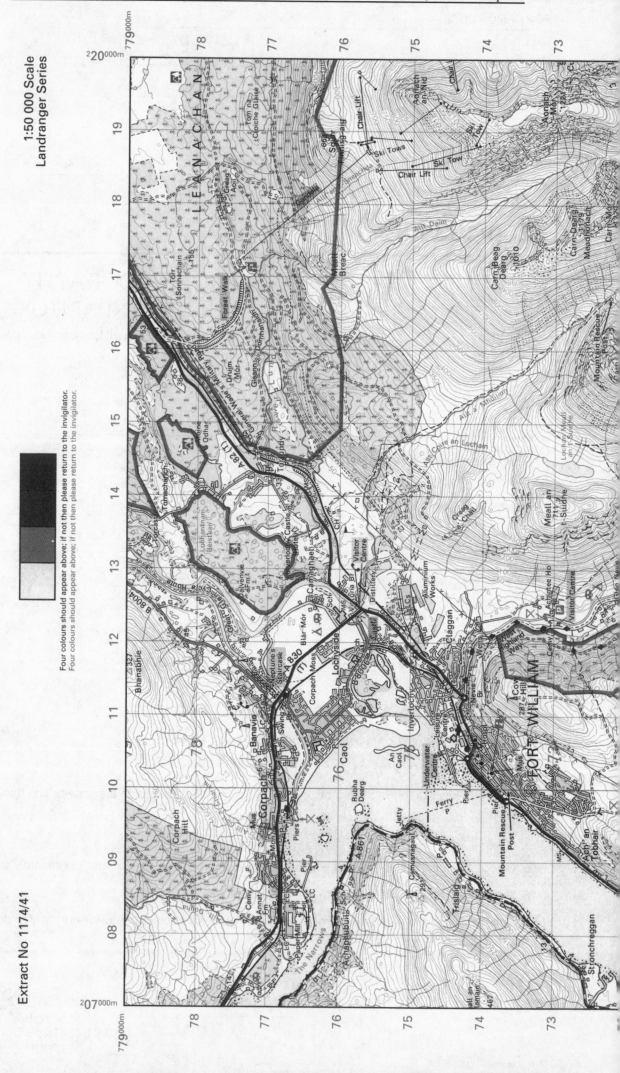

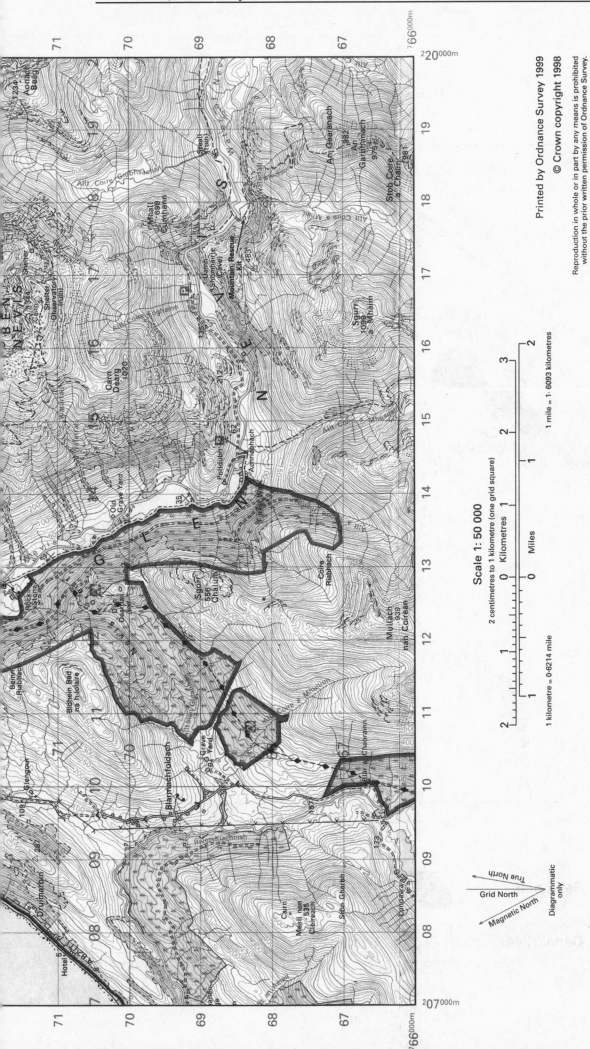

Scale 1: 50 000

2 centimetres to 1 kilometre (one grid square)

Printed by Ordnance Survey 1999

© Crown copyright 1998

Reproduction in whole or in part by any means is prohibited
without the prior written permission of Ordnance Survey.

1 kilometre = 0·6214 mile

1 mile = 1· 6093 kilometres

True North
Grid North
Magnetic North
Diagrammatic
only

1.

Reference Diagram Q1A

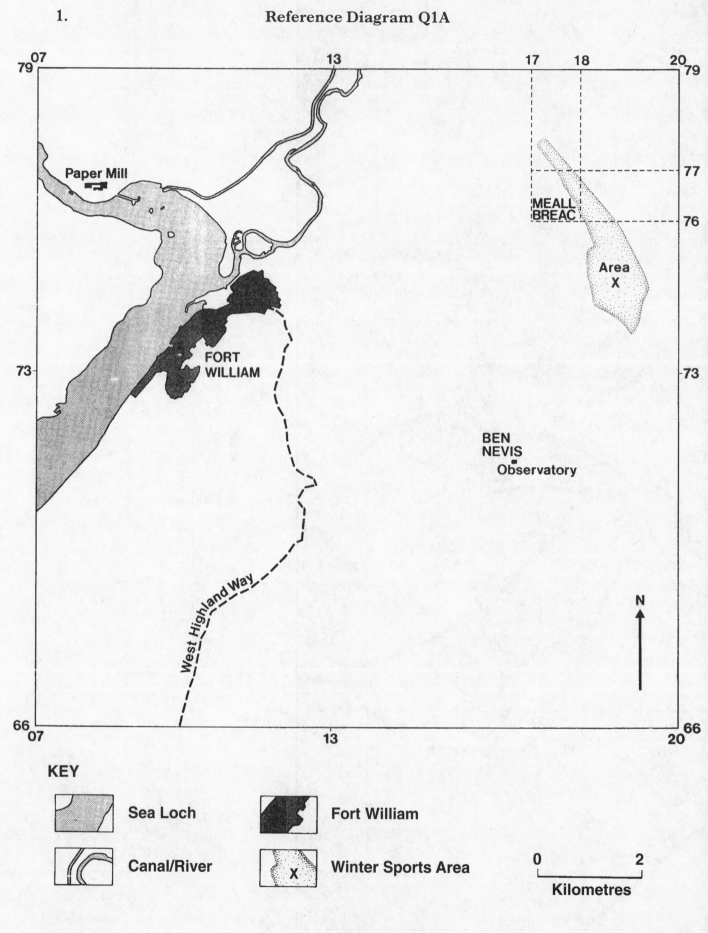

KEY

Sea Loch	Fort William
Canal/River	Winter Sports Area (X)

0   2
Kilometres

Marks

1. (continued)

Look at the Ordnance Survey Map Extract (No 1174/41) of the Fort William area and Reference Diagram Q1A on *Page two*.

(a) Using map evidence, describe the advantages **and** disadvantages of the site of Fort William.

Advantages _____

_____

_____

_____

Disadvantages _____

_____

_____

_____

4

(b) Area X on Reference Diagram Q1A has been developed for skiing.

Using map evidence, **describe** the likely effects this has had on the area covered by the whole map extract.

_____

_____

_____

_____

_____

_____

_____

4

[Turn over

Marks

1. (continued)

**Reference Diagram Q1B: An Aerial View looking south from above
Meall Breac (1776)**

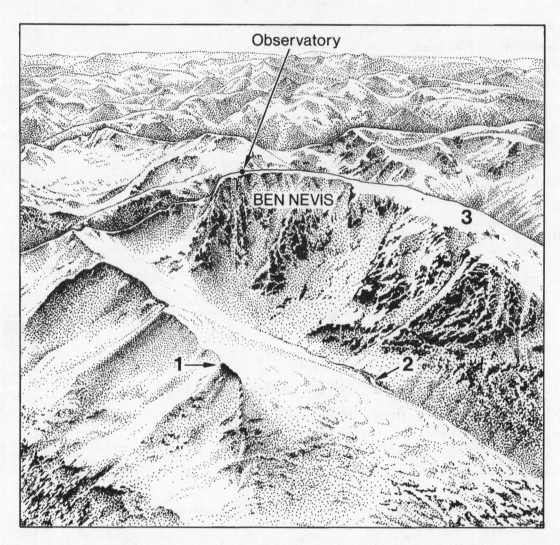

(c) Look at Reference Diagram Q1A, Reference Diagram Q1B and the map extract.

Identify the three features marked 1, 2 and 3.

Choose from:

Allt a Mhuilinn, Sgurr a Mhaim, Carn Beag Dearg, Carn Dearg.

1 _____

2 _____

3 _____   3

Marks

1. (continued)

(d)   Match each of the glacial features in the table below to the correct grid square.

Grid squares: 1869   1674   1272   1771

Glacial Features	Grid Square
Arête	
Hanging Valley	
"U" Shaped Valley	

3

(e)   **Explain** how **one** of the glacial features listed in (d) was formed. You may use a sketch to illustrate your answer.

_____

_____

_____

_____

_____

_____

_____

_____

_____

_____

3

[Turn over

Marks

1. (continued)

   (*f*)   There is a large paper mill in grid square 0876.

        Explain why this site is a suitable location for the paper mill. You **must** use map evidence.

_____

_____

_____

_____

_____

_____

4

Marks

1. (continued)

Reference Diagram Q1C: Erosion along the West Highland Way

(g) Look at Reference Diagram Q1C above and the statement given below.

"Footpath erosion along the West Highland Way is now spoiling a beautiful landscape."

Give **two** gathering techniques which could be used when carrying out a study of footpath erosion.

Why are these techniques suitable?

_____

_____

_____

_____

_____

_____

_____

_____

4

Marks

2.   **Reference Diagram Q2: Weather Conditions in Scotland**
                                November 1995

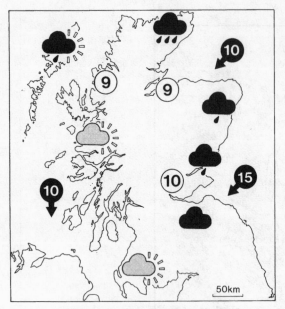

FRIDAY 9 NOVEMBER   SATURDAY 10 NOVEMBER

Key to Symbols

9 Temperature in degrees celsius	**Thin cloud**	☼ Sunny	**Light rain or drizzle**
15 Wind speed and direction	**Thick cloud**	Sunny spells	**Rain**

Look at Reference Diagram Q2.

Compare Friday's weather with Saturday's weather along the **east** coast of Scotland. You must refer to **more than one** weather element.

_____

_____

_____

_____

_____

_____

_____

4

Marks

3.   **Reference Diagram Q3: Land Uses in the Countryside**

Look at Reference Diagram Q3.

"There are possible conflicts between the land uses shown."

Do you agree with the above statement?

Tick (✓) the box.   YES ☐   NO ☐

Explain your answer.

_____

_____

_____

_____

_____

_____

_____

4

Marks

4.   **Reference Diagram Q4: Climate Graph for Athens (Greece)**

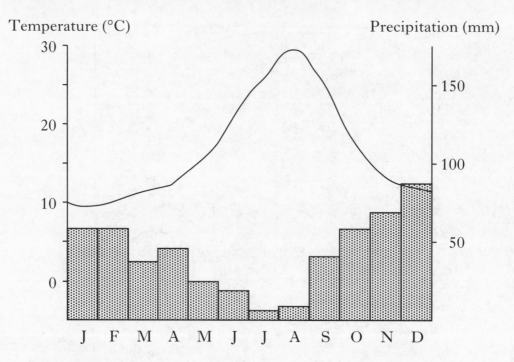

Temperature (°C)   Precipitation (mm)

(a) **Describe** in detail the climate shown in Reference Diagram Q4.

_____

_____

_____

_____   **3**

(b) What are the likely advantages **and** disadvantages of the climate
     shown in Reference Diagram Q4 for **people** living in areas which have
     this type of climate?

     Advantages _____

     _____

     _____

     _____

     Disadvantages _____

     _____

     _____

     _____   **4**

5.   **Reference Diagram Q5: Greater Manchester**

Reference Diagram Q5: Greater Manchester

Look at Reference Diagram Q5.

(a)   **Describe** the way Manchester has grown since 1850.

_____

_____

_____

_____

_____

3

(b)   **Describe** the methods used to limit the growth of large urban areas
       such as Greater Manchester.

_____

_____

_____

_____

_____

4

Marks

6.   **Reference Diagram Q6: Recent Developments in Agriculture**

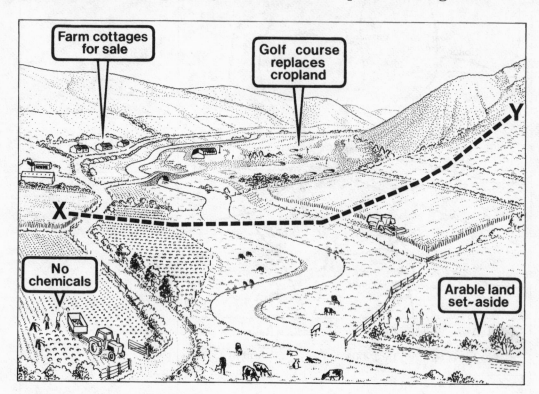

Look at Reference Diagram Q6.

(a) Choose **two** of the developments in agriculture shown in the above diagram and give reasons why each one is taking place.

Development _____

Explanation _____

_____

_____

_____

_____

Development _____

Explanation _____

_____

_____

_____

_____

4

Marks

6. (continued)

(*b*) Information has been gathered along line **X–Y** on land use and height. What technique would you use to show this information?

Give reasons for your choice of technique.

_____

_____

_____

_____

_____

_____

3

[Turn over

7.   **Reference Diagram Q7: Developing World Migration Model**

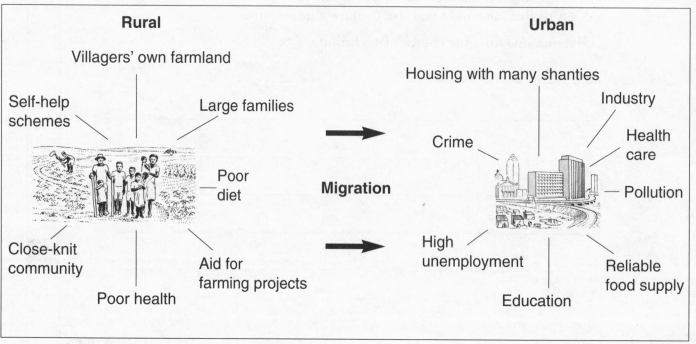

Marks

"Migration is always a move to better opportunities."

Do you agree with the statement?

Tick (✓) your choice.   YES ☐   NO ☐

Give reasons for your choice.

_____

_____

_____

_____

_____

_____

_____

_____

4

Marks

8. (*a*) A population pyramid for France is drawn below (Reference Diagram Q8A).

Reference Diagram Q8A

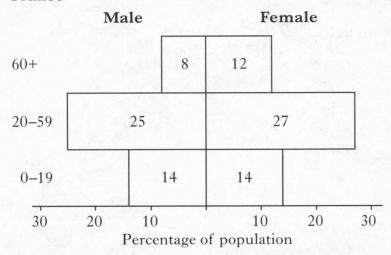

France

Reference Table Q8B: Age Structure of Population

	Age Groups	Male % of population	Female % of population
	60+	3	3
Nigeria	20–59	19	18
	0–19	28	29

Reference Diagram Q8C

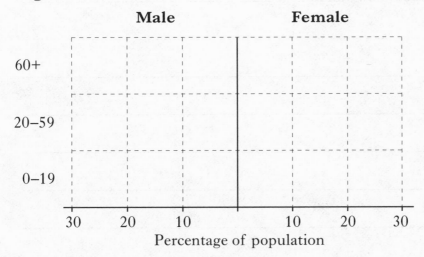

Nigeria

Use the information in Reference Table Q8B to complete the population pyramid for Nigeria (Reference Diagram Q8C).

3

Marks

8. (continued)

Reference Diagram Q8D: Life Expectancy

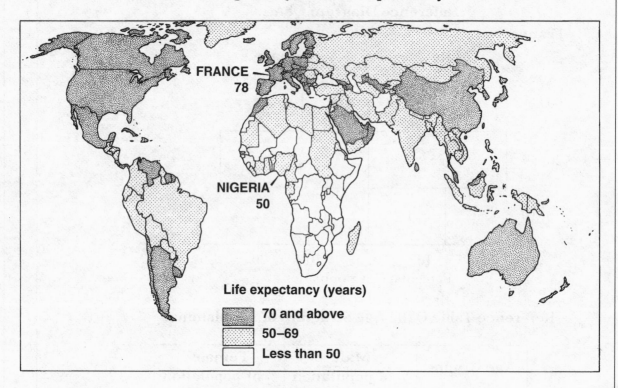

(b)   Look at Reference Diagram Q8D above.

Explain why Life Expectancy is higher in France than in Nigeria.

_____

_____

_____

_____

_____

_____

_____

_____

_____

4

Marks

9.   **Reference Diagram Q9: Hurricane Disaster in Central America**

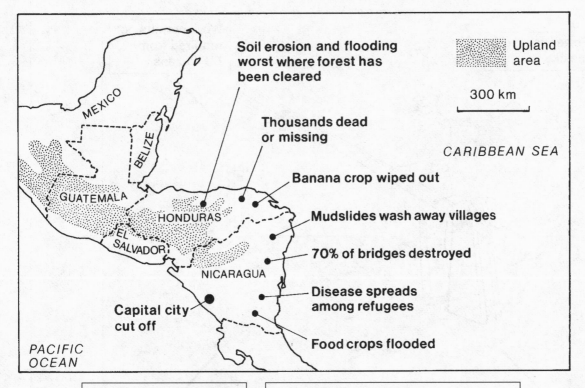

Soil erosion and flooding
worst where forest has
been cleared

Upland
area

300 km

Thousands dead
or missing

CARIBBEAN SEA

Banana crop wiped out

Mudslides wash away villages

70% of bridges destroyed

Disease spreads
among refugees

Capital city
cut off

Food crops flooded

MEXICO

BELIZE

GUATEMALA

HONDURAS

EL
SALVADOR

NICARAGUA

*PACIFIC
OCEAN*

• **Short Term Aid**	• **Long Term Aid**
deals with the most urgent problems	aid which rebuilds and develops a country over several years

Look at Reference Diagram Q9.

> "Only short term aid can help Central America recover from Hurricane
> Mitch." (UN Spokesperson 1998)

Do you agree with the statement?

Tick (✓) your choice.   YES ☐   NO ☐

Give reasons for your choice.

Reasons _____

_____

_____

_____

_____

_____

4

Marks

10.   **Reference Diagram Q10: Europe's Open Borders**

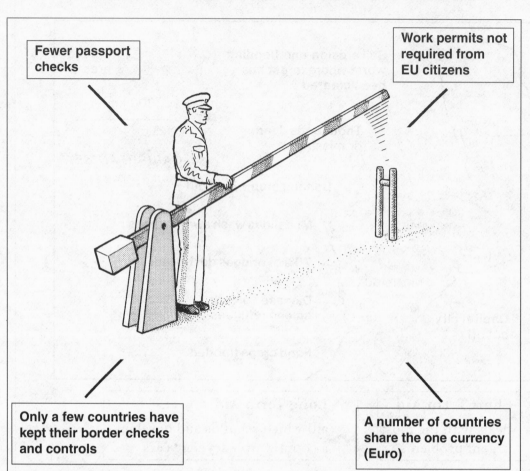

Fewer passport checks

Work permits not required from EU citizens

Only a few countries have kept their border checks and controls

A number of countries share the one currency (Euro)

Look at Reference Diagram Q10 which shows new arrangements for EU member countries.

Explain the advantages of the new arrangements to the people living in the European Union.

_____

_____

_____

_____

_____   4

[END OF QUESTION PAPER]

[BLANK PAGE]

[BLANK PAGE]

G

FOR OFFICIAL USE

KU   ES

Total Marks

1260/403

NATIONAL   WEDNESDAY, 23 MAY   **GEOGRAPHY**
QUALIFICATIONS   **G/C** 9.00 AM – 10.25 AM   **STANDARD GRADE**
2001   **F/G** 10.25 AM – 11.50 AM   General Level

Fill in these boxes and read what is printed below.

Full name of centre   Town

Forename(s)   Surname

Date of birth
Day Month Year   Scottish candidate number   Number of seat

1 Read the whole of each question carefully before you answer it.

2 Write in the spaces provided.

3 Where boxes like this ☐ are provided, put a tick ✓ in the box beside the answer you think is correct.

4 Try all the questions.

5 Do not give up the first time you get stuck: you may be able to answer later questions.

6 Extra paper may be obtained from the invigilator, if required.

7 Before leaving the examination room you must give this book to the invigilator. If you do not, you may lose all the marks for this paper.

SCOTTISH
QUALIFICATIONS
AUTHORITY

©

Extract No 1212/64

1:50 000 Scale
Landranger Series

Four colours should appear above; if not then please return to the invigilator.
Four colours should appear above; if not then please return to the invigilator.

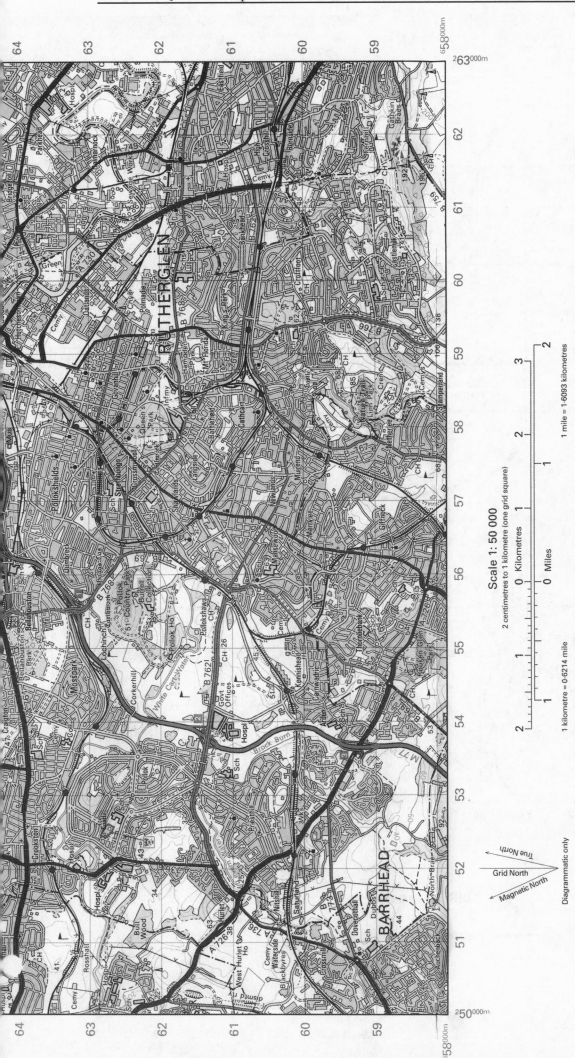

Scale 1: 50 000

2 centimetres to 1 kilometre (one grid square)

1 mile = 1·6093 kilometres

1 kilometre = 0·6214 mile

1.   **Reference Diagram Q1A**

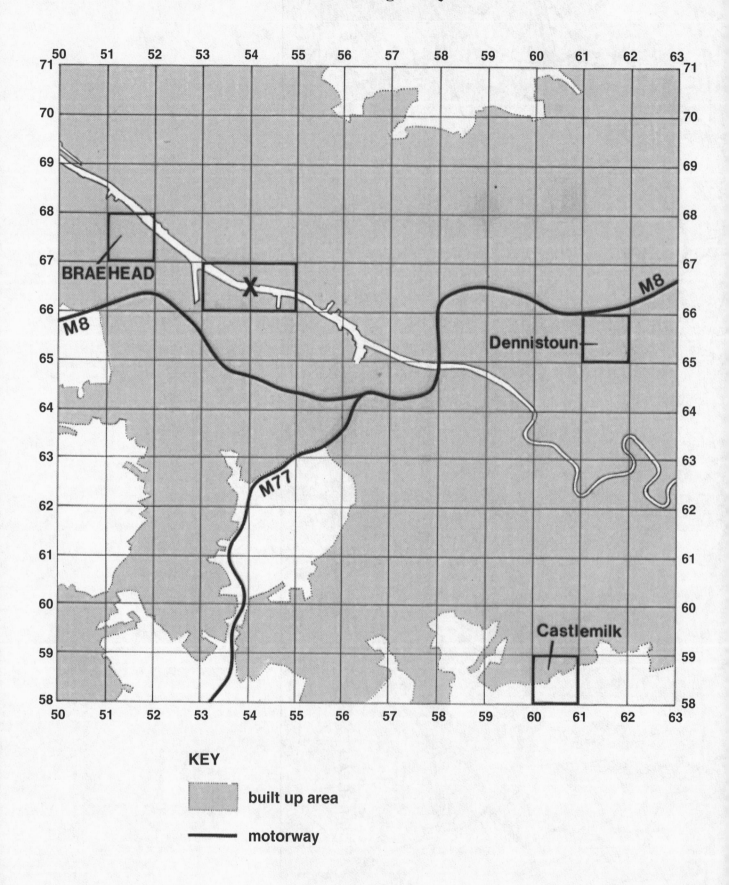

KEY

built up area

motorway

Marks

1. (continued)

Look at the Ordnance Survey Map Extract (No 1212/64) of the central Glasgow area and Reference Diagram Q1A on *Page two*.

(*a*)   Dennistoun (6165) and Castlemilk (6058) are both residential areas.

Using **map evidence**, describe the **differences** between these two areas.

_____

_____

_____

_____

_____   **4**

(*b*)   **Reference Diagram Q1B: Braehead Shopping Centre**

Reference Diagram Q1B shows the recently built shopping centre at Braehead (5167).

Using **map evidence**, give reasons why it was built at this location.

_____

_____

_____

_____   **4**

[Turn over

Marks

1. (continued)

   (*c*)   Look at Reference Diagram Q1A and the map extract.

        Give **map evidence** to show that area X (5366 and 5466), shown on Reference Diagram Q1A, is an industrial zone.

_____

_____

_____

_____

_____

4

   (*d*)   Reference Diagram Q1A shows the extension to the M77, opened in 1997.

        Using **map evidence**, give the advantages **and** disadvantages of this new motorway.

Advantages _____

_____

_____

_____

Disadvantages _____

_____

_____

4

Marks

1. (continued)

(*e*) **Reference Text Q1C:
Selected Human Activities on River Clyde**

- Industry

- Communications

- Housing

- Recreation

Look at Reference Text Q1C and the map extract.

In what ways has the River Clyde both encouraged **and** restricted human activities in Glasgow?

_____

_____

_____

_____

_____   **4**

[Turn over

[BLANK PAGE]

KU | ES

Marks

2.   **Reference Diagram Q2: Ox-Bow Lake**

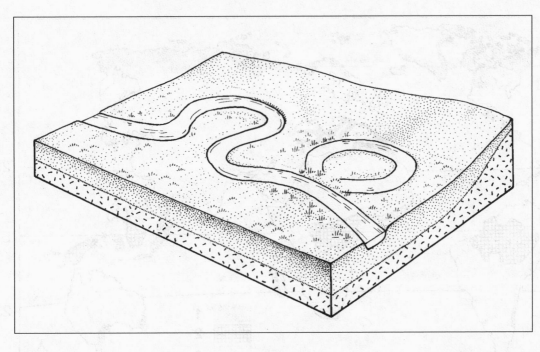

Explain how an ox-bow lake is formed.

You may use diagrams to illustrate your answer.

_____

_____

_____

_____

_____

_____

_____

_____

_____

3

[Turn over

3.   **Reference Diagram Q3A: Selected Climate Regions**

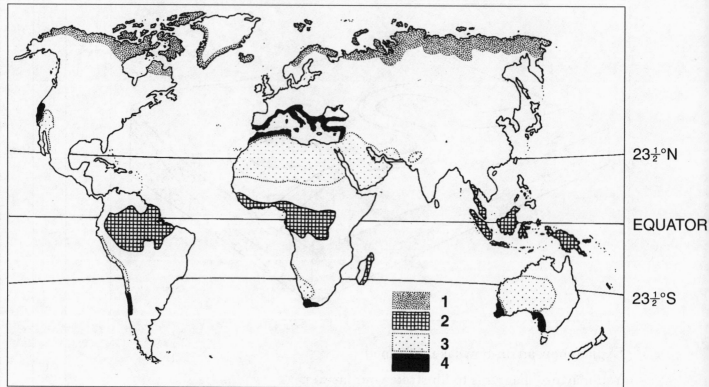

Marks

(*a*)   Look at Reference Diagram Q3A.

Complete the table below by naming the climate regions **1** to **4** shown on the map.

Choose from:

Mediterranean, Tundra, Hot Desert, Equatorial Rain Forest.

Number	Climate Region
1	
2	
3	
4	

3

KU | ES

Marks

3. (continued)

Reference Diagram Q3B: Climate Graph

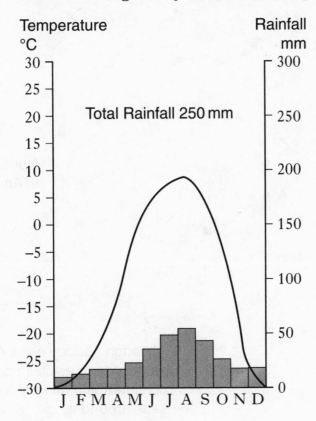

(b)   Look at Reference Diagram Q3B.

The climate graph shows one of the four climates shown on Reference Diagram Q3A.

(i)   Identify the climate shown by the graph.

Climate _____

1

(ii)   Give reasons for your choice.

Reasons _____

_____

_____

_____

_____

2

[Turn over

4.

Reference Diagram Q4A: Antarctica

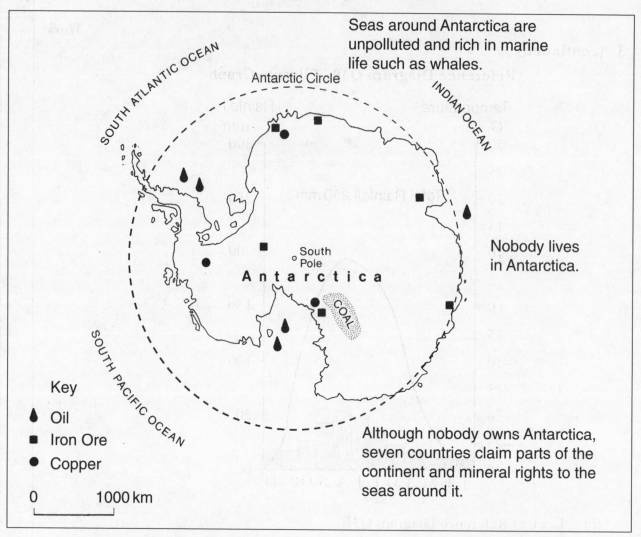

Seas around Antarctica are unpolluted and rich in marine life such as whales.

Antarctic Circle

SOUTH ATLANTIC OCEAN

INDIAN OCEAN

SOUTH PACIFIC OCEAN

South Pole

A n t a r c t i c a

COAL

Nobody lives in Antarctica.

Although nobody owns Antarctica, seven countries claim parts of the continent and mineral rights to the seas around it.

Key

♦ Oil
■ Iron Ore
● Copper

0   1000 km

Reference Diagram Q4B: Different Views about the Antarctic Region

There's a serious world shortage of oil.
We must get access to this area's huge oil and coal reserves.

Under no circumstances should we allow mining or oil companies to plunder this area's resources.

SAVE THE WHALES

Multinational Oil Company

Environmental Organisation

Marks

4. (continued)

Look at Reference Diagrams Q4A and Q4B.

Do you think Antarctica's mineral resources should be developed?

Give reasons for your answer.

Tick (✓) your choice.   YES ☐   NO ☐

Reasons _____

_____

_____

_____

_____

_____

4

[Turn over

5.   **Reference Diagram Q5A: Farming Landscape in 1950**

Small irregular fields

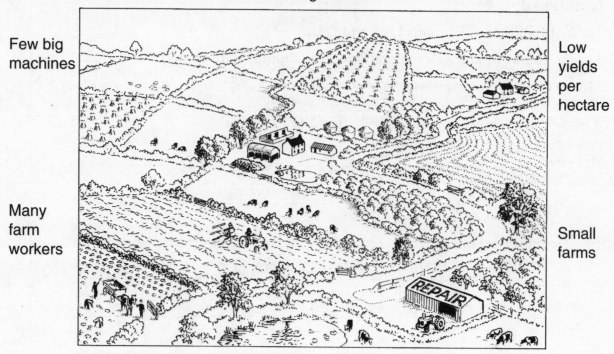

Few big machines

Low yields per hectare

Many farm workers

Small farms

Reference Diagram Q5B: Farming Landscape in 2000

Large regular fields

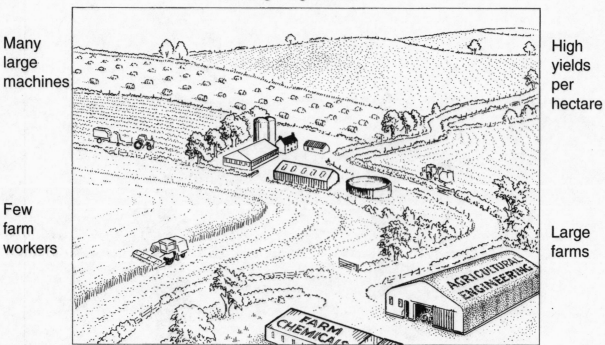

Many large machines

High yields per hectare

Few farm workers

Large farms

Marks

5. (continued)

(*a*) Look at Reference Diagrams Q5A and Q5B.

What are the advantages **and** disadvantages of the changes which have taken place in farming since 1950?

Advantages _____

_____

_____

_____

Disadvantages _____

_____

_____

_____

4

[Turn over

KU | ES

Marks

5. (continued)

Reference Table Q5C: Farm Information collected by Student

Field Number	Field Size (hectares)	Slope Steepness (degrees)	Land Use
1	5	2	barley
2	7	12	permanent grass
3	8	4	potatoes
4	12	6	barley
5	13	20	rough grazing

Reference Diagram Q5D: Map of Fields on Farm

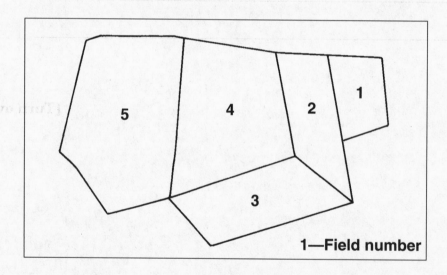

1—**Field number**

(b)   Look at Reference Table Q5C and Reference Diagram Q5D.

Choose two **different** techniques to process the farm data that the student has collected.

Technique 1 _____

Technique 2 _____

Justify your choices. _____

_____

_____

_____

4

6.   **Reference Diagram Q6: Ben Lawers Area**

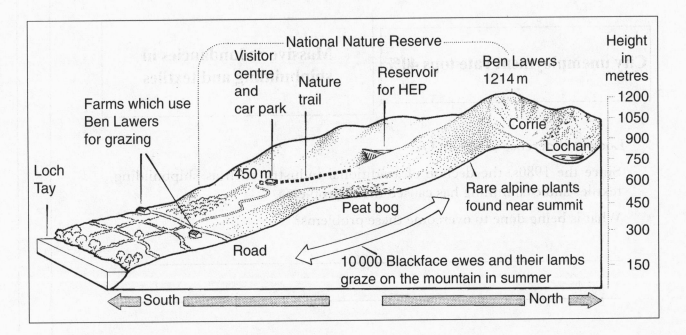

Look at Reference Diagram Q6.

(a) Many people visit Ben Lawers. What problems might this create for the area?

Marks

_____

_____

_____

_____

4

(b) A group of secondary pupils is to investigate the relationship between land use and height on Ben Lawers.

Describe **two** techniques which they could use to collect appropriate data.

Technique 1 _____

Technique 2 _____

Justify your choices. _____

_____

_____

_____

4

Marks

7.   **Reference Diagram Q7: Newspaper Headlines of the 1980s**

City unemployment rate tops 40%	Massive redundancies in shipbuilding and textiles

Look at Reference Diagram Q7.

Since the 1980s, the decline of traditional industry such as shipbuilding, textiles and coal mining has caused many problems.

What is being done to overcome these problems?

_____

_____

_____

_____

_____   **3**

Marks

8. **Reference Diagram Q8: Projected Changes in World Population**

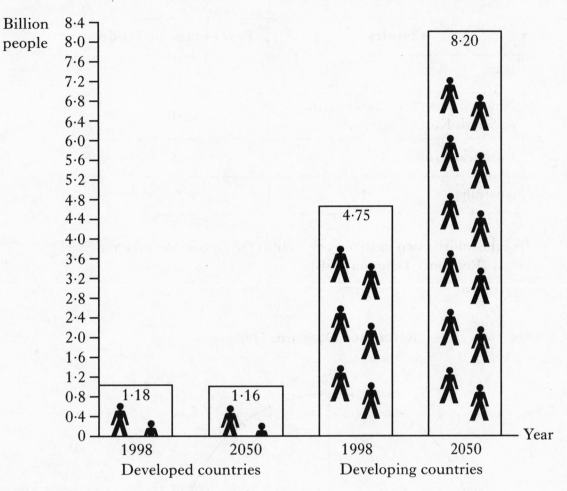

(a) Look at Reference Diagram Q8.

Describe in detail the changes in population predicted for the developed and developing countries.

_____

_____

_____

_____

4

(b) Describe the problems which **developing** countries are likely to have as a result of the changes in their population.

_____

_____

_____

_____

4

Page seventeen **[Turn over**

Marks

9. (*a*)   **Reference Table Q9A: Japan—Main Export Partners**

Country	Percentage of Trade
USA	80
Newly industrialised countries, eg South Korea	10
European Union	5
Australia	5

Use the information in Reference Table Q9A to complete the pie chart below (Reference Diagram Q9B).

3

Reference Diagram Q9B

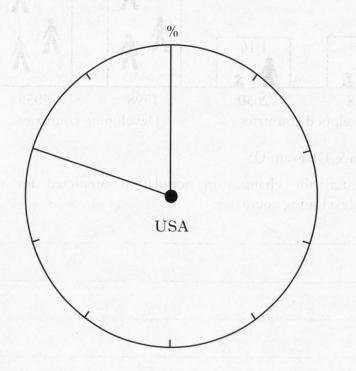

USA

KU | ES

Marks

9. (continued)

(b)   **Reference Table Q9C: Japan—Key Statistics**

Selected Exports	World Rank
Car Manufacturing	1
Computer Chips	1
Telecommunications	1
Shipbuilding	3
Iron and Steel	3

Population (millions) 2000	130
Population (world rank)	7
GNP (world rank)	2

Look at the Reference Table Q9C.

Give reasons why Japan is one of the world's economic superpowers.

_____

_____

_____

_____

_____   **4**

[Turn over for Question 10 on *Page twenty*

Marks

10.   **Reference Text Q10A: Problems of a Village in Mali,
West Africa**

> - very few children go to school
> - mothers have to walk miles for water
> - most people cannot read or write
> - no rain, so the crops have died
> - many babies ill or dying of hunger

Reference Text Q10B: Selected Types of Aid

Send emergency food and medicine	Set up a local school with trained teachers	Provide irrigation scheme
A	B	C

Look at Reference Texts Q10A and Q10B above.

What type of aid do you think would be most suited to this village?

Tick (✓) your choice.

A ☐   B ☐   C ☐

Give reasons for your answer.

_____

_____

_____

_____

4

[END OF QUESTION PAPER]

1260/105

SCOTTISH
CERTIFICATE OF
EDUCATION
1997

TUESDAY, 13 MAY
1.00 PM – 2.45 PM

GEOGRAPHY
STANDARD GRADE
Credit Level

All questions should be attempted.

Candidates should read the questions carefully.   Answers should be clearly expressed and relevant.

Credit will always be given for appropriate sketch-maps and diagrams.

Write legibly and neatly, and leave a space of about one cm between the lines.

Marks may be deducted for bad spelling and bad punctuation, and for writing that is difficult to read.

All maps and diagrams in this paper have been printed in black only: no other colours have been used.

SCOTTISH
QUALIFICATIONS
AUTHORITY
©   THB 1260/105 6/3/19160

1:50 000 Scale
Landranger Series

Extract No 1055/58

Four colours should appear above; if not then please return to the invigilator.

Scale 1:50 000

2 centimetres to 1 kilometre (one grid square)

Kilometres

Miles

1 kilometre = 0·6214 mile

1 mile = 1·6093 kilometres

Printed by Ordnance Survey 1996

© Crown copyright 1994

Reproduction in whole or in part by any means is prohibited without the prior permission of Ordnance Survey.

Map reproduced from Ordnance Survey mapping with the permission of the Controller of Her Majesty's Stationery Office, © Crown copyright, Licence No. 100036009.

1.   **Reference Diagram Q1A**

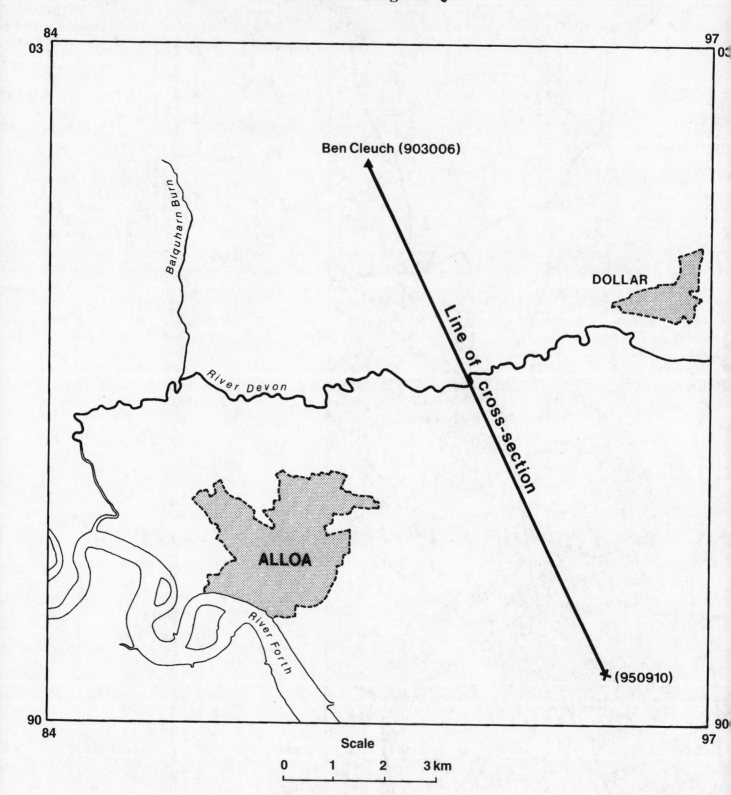

Marks

| KU | EV |

1. (continued)

This question refers to the OS Map Extract (No 1055/58) of the Alloa area, the Reference Diagram Q1A on page two and the Reference Diagram Q1B below.

Reference Diagram Q1B: Cross-section from GR 903006 to GR 950910

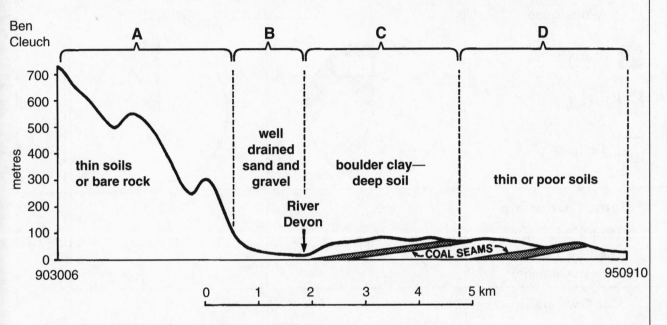

(a) Study the map extract and Reference Diagram Q1B above.

   Explain the differences in land use between areas **A**, **B**, **C** and **D**.   6

[Turn over

1. (continued)

Reference Diagram Q1C: Social Statistics for Alloa and Dollar (1991)

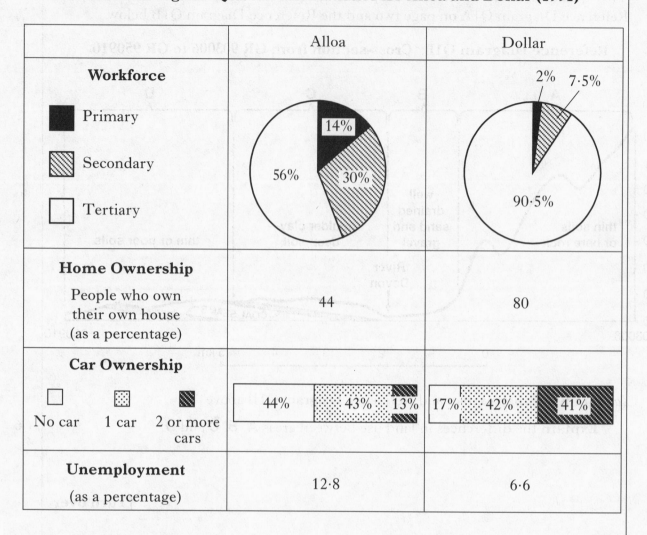

	Alloa	Dollar
Workforce ■ Primary ▨ Secondary ☐ Tertiary	56% 14% 30%	2% 7·5% 90·5%
Home Ownership People who own their own house (as a percentage)	44	80
Car Ownership ☐ No car ⊡ 1 car ▨ 2 or more cars	44% 43% 13%	17% 42% 41%
Unemployment (as a percentage)	12·8	6·6

Reference Text Q1D: Contrasting Settlement Functions

Some settlements grow as a result of manufacturing industry, whereas others may develop as "dormitories" with their residents working elsewhere.

(b) Consider the statement in Reference Text Q1D.

Referring to the data in Reference Diagram Q1C **and** map evidence, **explain** the different functions of Alloa and Dollar.

1. (continued)

Reference Diagram Q1E: Population Density of Alloa Map Extract

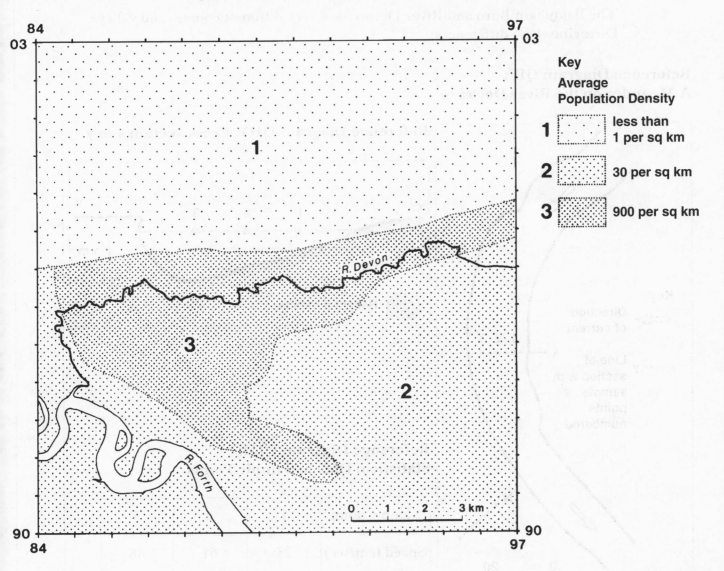

Key
Average
Population Density

1 — less than 1 per sq km

2 — 30 per sq km

3 — 900 per sq km

(c) Refer to Reference Diagram Q1E and the map extract.

Give possible reasons for differences in the population density between areas 1, 2 and 3.

	Marks	
	KU	EV
		4

[Turn over

Mark

KU

1. (continued)

(d) Look at Reference Diagram Q1A on page two and the Map Extract.

The Balquharn Burn and River Devon have very different courses and valleys. **Describe** these differences.

Reference Diagram Q1F:
A Meander on the River Devon

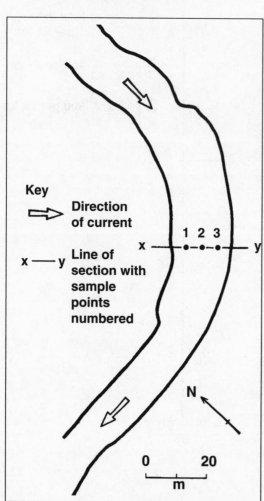

Reference Diagram Q1G: Cross-section x to y

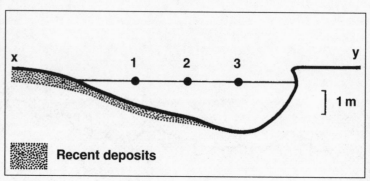

Recent deposits

Reference Diagram Q1H:
Statistical Data at Sample Points

Sample point	1	2	3
Speed (cm/sec)	25	61	88
Depth (m)	0·4	1·5	2·2

(e) Look at Reference Diagrams Q1F, Q1G and Q1H.

Explain the relationships between river speed, river depth, erosion and deposition.

Marks
KU | EV

2. **Reference Diagram Q2A: A Synoptic Chart**

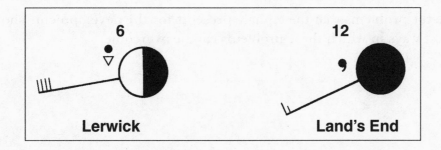

Tuesday 5th January 1993
1200 GMT

972

LERWICK

992

1008

1024

1032

LAND'S
END

Reference Diagram Q2B: Station Circles for 1200 hours on 5th January 1993

6

12

Lerwick

Land's End

Study Reference Diagrams Q2A and Q2B.

Explain in detail the differences in weather conditions at Lerwick and Land's End at that time.

4

[Turn over

3. **Reference Diagram Q3A: Climate Graph for North American Tundra (Cape Barron)**

Reference Diagram Q3B: Model of Land Use in North American Tundra

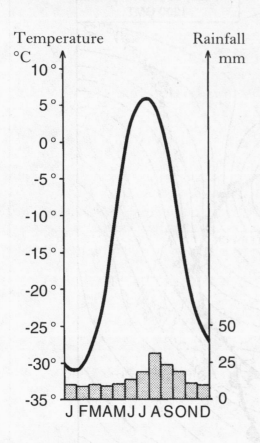

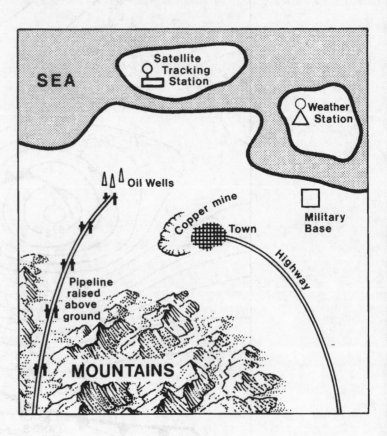

Marks
KU

(a) Study Reference Diagram Q3A.

Describe in detail the climate of Cape Barron.

(b) Study Reference Diagram Q3B.

Describe the problems that the climate presents for the developments shown and suggest ways in which these problems can be overcome.

4

4.   **Reference Text Q4A: Extract from Environmental Report**

"At the end of the twentieth century, industry and technology present an ever-increasing threat to the resources and environment of the seas and oceans of our planet. Urgent action is required by governments to prevent disaster."

Reference Diagram Q4B: Threats to the Seas and Oceans

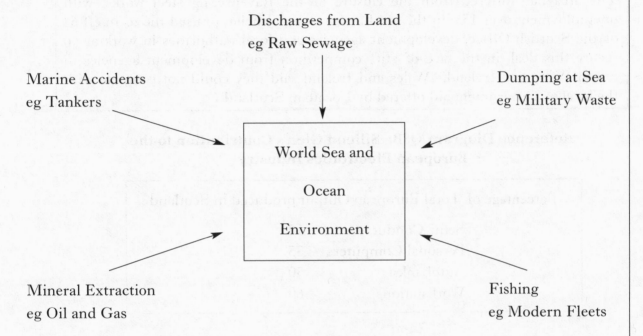

Discharges from Land
eg Raw Sewage

Marine Accidents
eg Tankers

Dumping at Sea
eg Military Waste

World Sea and

Ocean

Environment

Mineral Extraction
eg Oil and Gas

Fishing
eg Modern Fleets

Look at Reference Text Q4A and Reference Diagram Q4B.

Explain **in detail** why there should be so much concern about what is happening to the seas and oceans of the planet.

5

[Turn over

5.   **Reference Text Q5A: Taiwanese Picture Tube Company locates in Scotland**

> Chunghwa picture tubes, a Taiwanese electronics company has completed a £260 million investment in Silicon Glen. The factory to manufacture tubes for colour monitors will be built at Mossend, part of the Lanarkshire Enterprise Zone, and close to the Eurocentral Rail Freight Terminal. The factory will be completed by 1999 and should employ 1200 people. A further 1800 jobs should be created in spin off industries.
>
> The area has suffered from the closure of the Ravenscraig steel works, with unemployment over 15% in the local area. One politician praised the team effort of the Scottish Office, development agencies and local authorities in working to secure this deal, in the face of stiff competition from development agencies in South Wales and Ireland. Wales and Ireland said they could not compete with the level of Government aid offered by Locate in Scotland.

Reference Diagram Q5B: Silicon Glen's Contribution to the European Electronics Industry

Percentage of Total European Output produced in Scotland

Semi-Conductors	12
Personal Computers	35
Autobanks	50
Workstations	60

Reference Diagram Q5C: Distribution of Electronics Factories in Silicon Glen

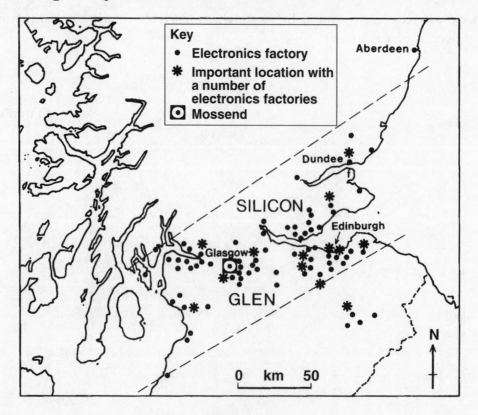

5. (continued)

Reference Diagram Q5D: Location of Silicon Glen in UK

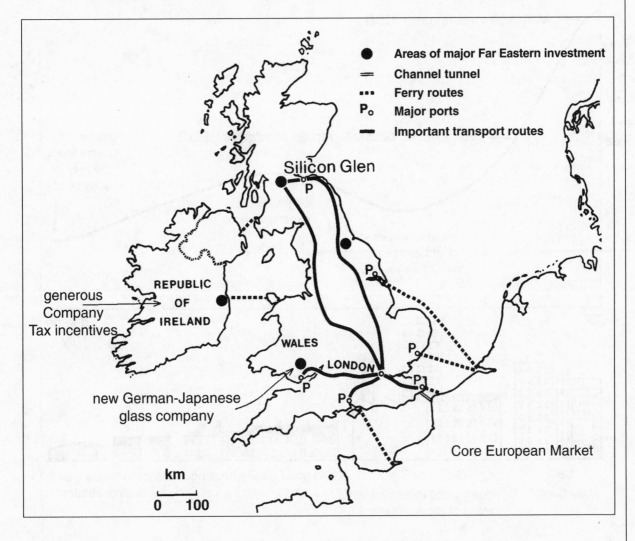

Look at Reference Text Q5A and Reference Diagrams Q5B, Q5C and Q5D.

What were the advantages **and** disadvantages for the Chunghwa Company of locating at the Mossend site in the Silicon Glen area?

6

[Turn over

6.   **Reference Diagram Q6: Urban Transect**

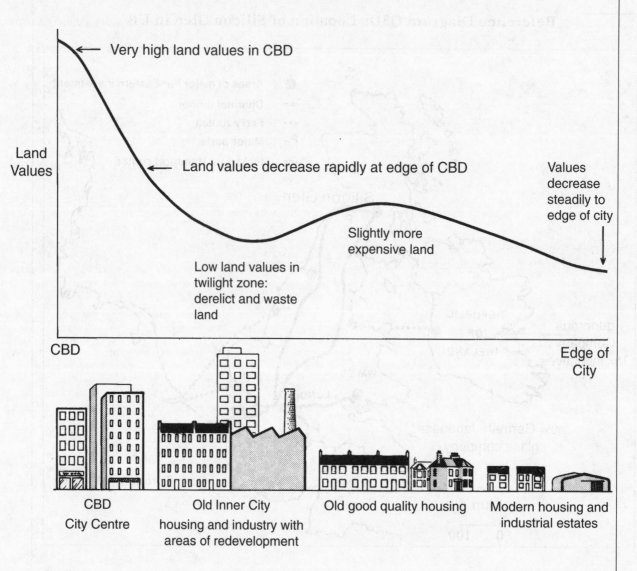

Cities have grown outwards from the city centre.

Look at Reference Diagram Q6 and **explain** the changes in urban land use **from** the CBD **to** the edge of the city.

You may refer to examples you have studied in the UK.

6

Marks

KU	EV

7. **Reference Diagram Q7: Population Pyramids for Japan and Bangladesh**

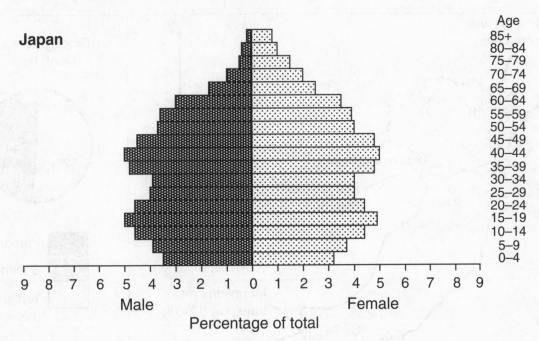

Japan

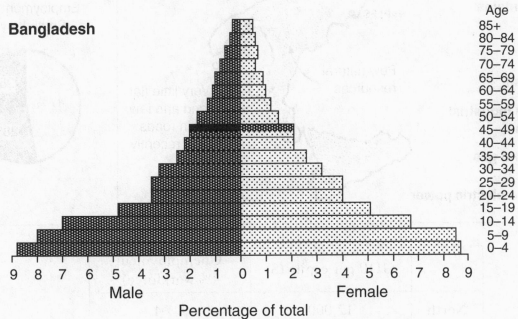

Bangladesh

Study Reference Diagram Q7 above.

(a) **Describe** the differences between the population structures of Japan and Bangladesh.

3

(b) Give reasons for the differences shown.

6

[Turn over

8.   **Reference Diagram Q8: Italy North and South**

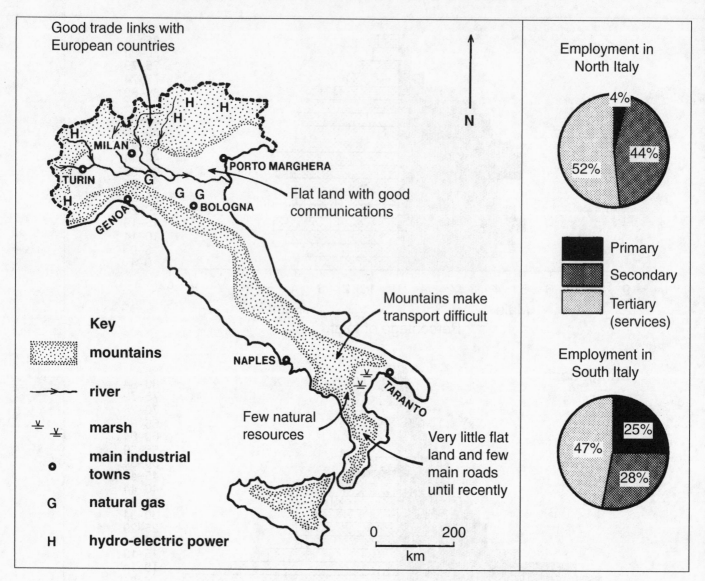

	GDP per capita ($)	Unemployment (% workforce)
North	12,000	7·1
South	6,500	21·4

The South of Italy receives more assistance from the European Union than the North. A North Italian politician recently stated:

"This is most unfair. Italy is **one** country and the North should receive as much as the South."

Do you agree with the politician? **Explain** your answer using the information in Reference Diagram Q8.

Mark

KU

Marks

KU	EV

9.   **Reference Diagram Q9: Share of World's Exports**

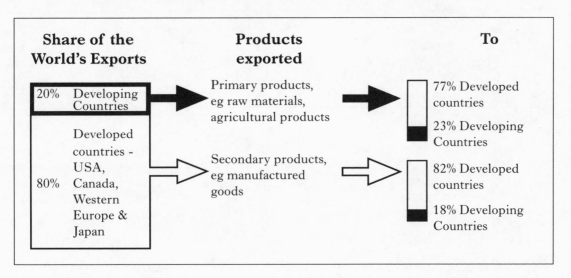

Look at Reference Diagram Q9.

Explain why certain countries of the World dominate World Trade.   4

[END OF QUESTION PAPER]

[BLANK PAGE]

C

1260/105

SCOTTISH
CERTIFICATE OF
EDUCATION
1998

TUESDAY, 12 MAY
10.30 AM – 12.15 PM

GEOGRAPHY
STANDARD GRADE
Credit Level

All questions should be attempted.

Candidates should read the questions carefully. Answers should be clearly expressed and relevant.

Credit will always be given for appropriate sketch-maps and diagrams.

Write legibly and neatly, and leave a space of about one cm between the lines.

Marks may be deducted for bad spelling and bad punctuation, and for writing that is difficult to read.

All maps and diagrams in this paper have been printed in black only: no other colours have been used.

SCOTTISH
QUALIFICATIONS
AUTHORITY

Extract No 1101/171

1:50 000 Scale
Landranger Series

Four colours should appear above; if not then please return to the invigilator.

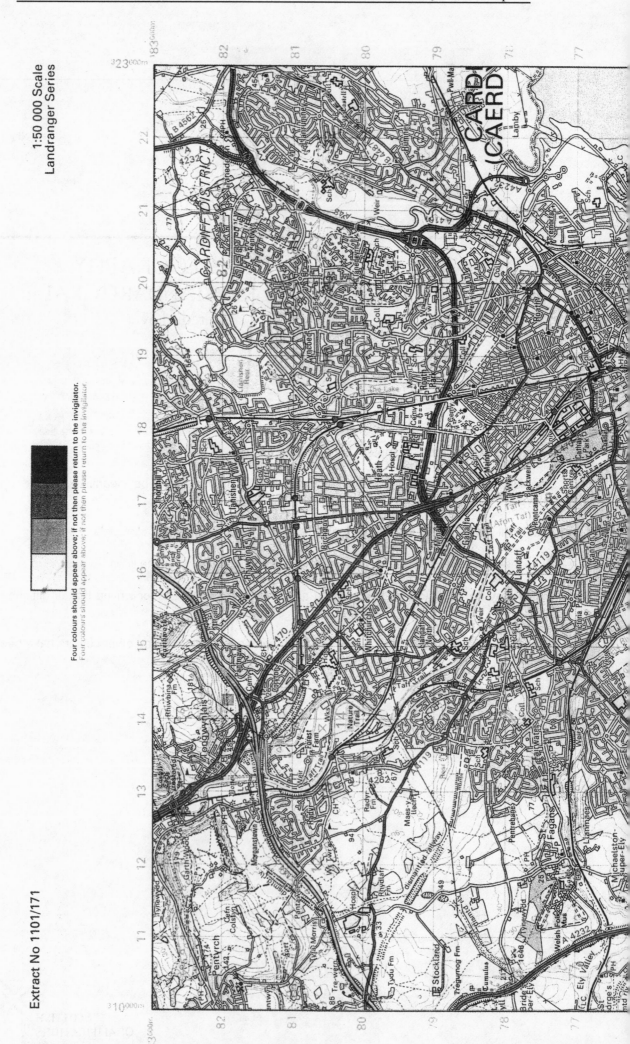

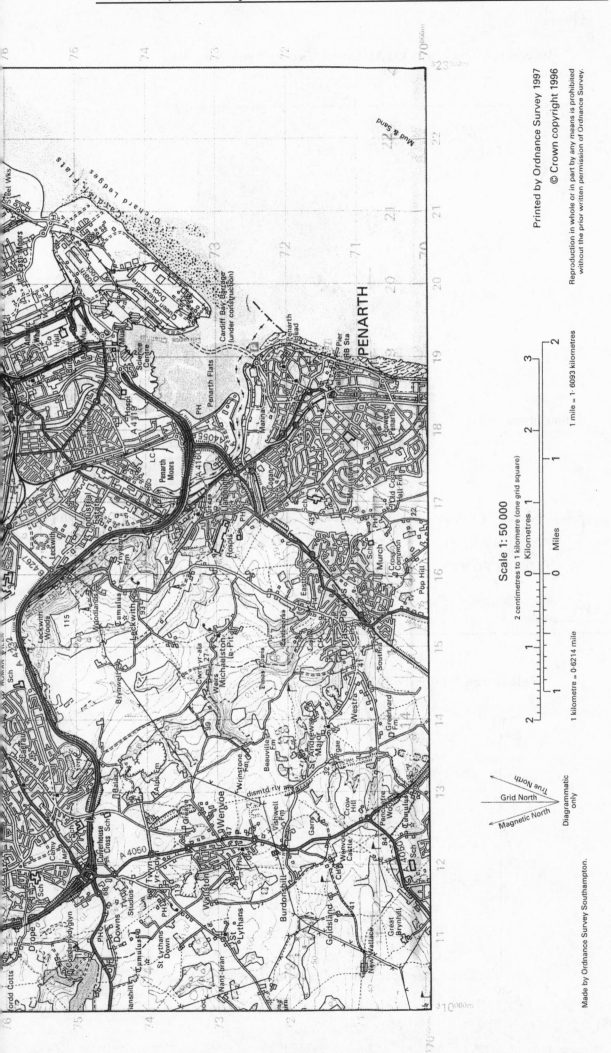

Scale 1 : 50 000

2 centimetres to 1 kilometre (one grid square)

1 mile = 1·6093 kilometres

1 kilometre = 0·6214 mile

Diagrammatic
only

True North

Grid North

Magnetic North

Made by Ordnance Survey Southampton.

1.

Reference Diagram Q1A: Land Use in Area X in 1966

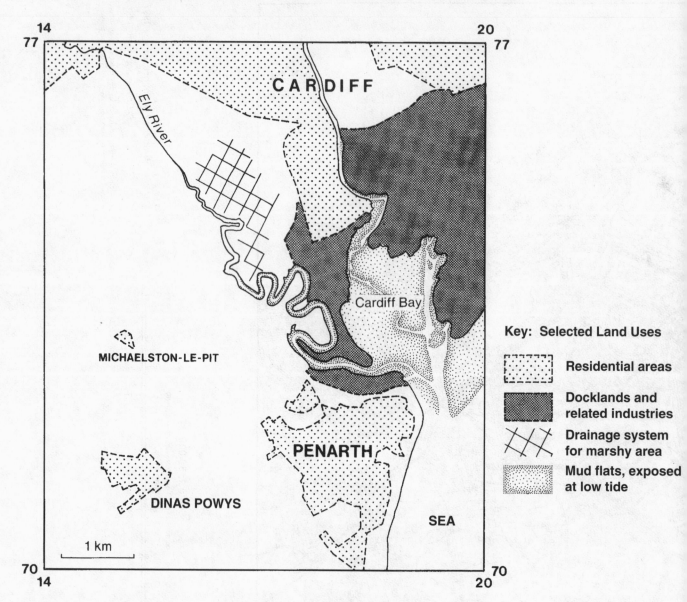

Key: Selected Land Uses

- Residential areas
- Docklands and related industries
- Drainage system for marshy area
- Mud flats, exposed at low tide

Reference Diagram Q1B: Location of Area X

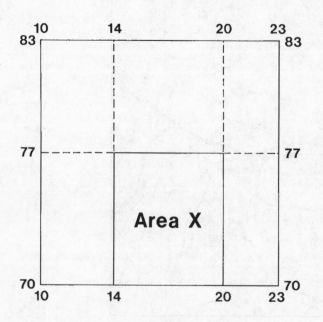

Marks

| KU | EV |

1. (continued)

This question refers to the OS Map Extract (No 1101/171) of Cardiff and Reference Diagrams Q1A and Q1B on Page two.

Look at Reference Diagrams Q1A and Q1B.

(a) Find Area **X** on the OS map extract.

Using map evidence, **describe** the changes in urban and industrial land use in Area **X** since 1966.

6

(b) The main present day functions of the Cardiff area are tourism and recreation.

Do you agree with this statement? Use map evidence to support your answer.

4

Reference Diagram Q1C: Aerial View looking NW from 210710

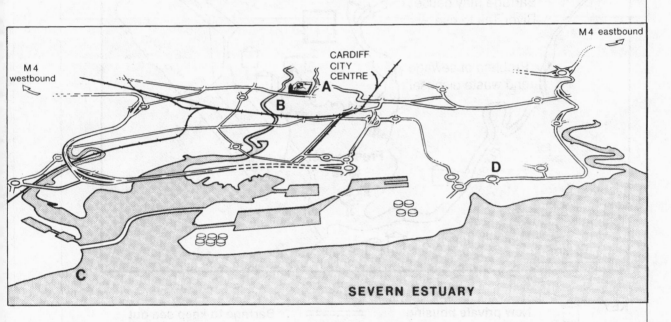

(c) Look at Reference Diagram Q1C and the map extract.

Identify the four features marked **A**, **B**, **C** and **D**.

Choose from:

Penarth Head; Queen Alexandra Dock; Steel Works; Civic Centre; Stadium.

3

(d) Radyr Farm (130798) is close to a built up area.

Using map evidence, give the advantages **and** disadvantages of this farm's location.

4

[Turn over

1. (continued)

Reference Diagram Q1D: Cardiff Bay Barrage Scheme

The **Barrage** is a barrier 1·1 km long being built to keep the sea out of Cardiff Bay and Penarth Flats. The area will be landscaped and a 200 hectare freshwater lake will be formed.

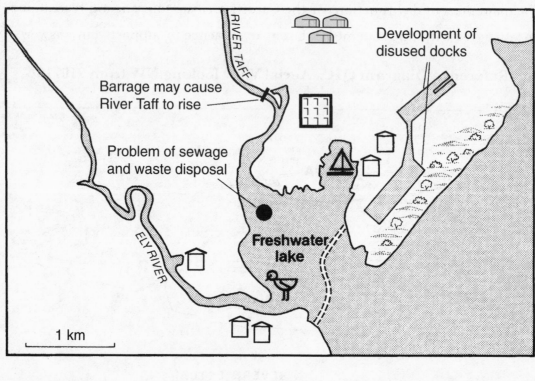

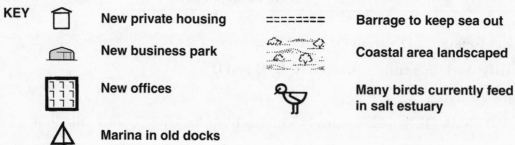

KEY

🏠 New private housing

🏭 New business park

🔳 New offices

⛵ Marina in old docks

======== Barrage to keep sea out

Coastal area landscaped

🐦 Many birds currently feed in salt estuary

(e) Look at Reference Diagram Q1D and the map extract.

Explain the advantages **and** disadvantages of the Cardiff Bay Barrage Scheme and related developments.

2. **Reference Diagram Q2A: An Area of Glacial Erosion**

Pyramidal Peak

Reference Diagram Q2B: An Area of Glacial Deposition

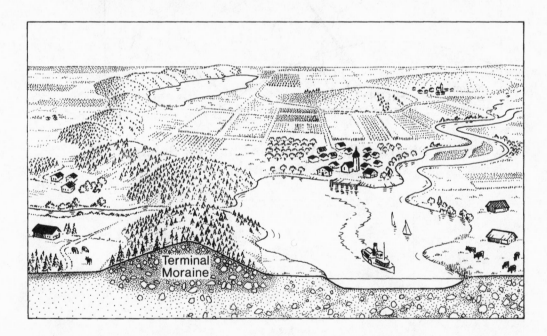

Terminal Moraine

Look at the Reference Diagrams above.

(a) **Explain** how **either** a pyramidal peak **or** a terminal moraine is formed.   **4**

(b) Give reasons why land use **differs** between areas of glacial erosion and glacial deposition.   **6**

[Turn over

3.   **Reference Diagram Q3A: European Synoptic Chart for noon
Wednesday 6 November 1996**

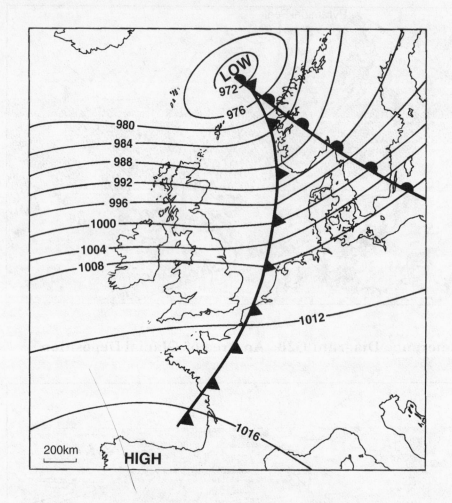

**Reference Diagram Q3B: Weather Chart for Scotland on
Wednesday 6 November 1996**

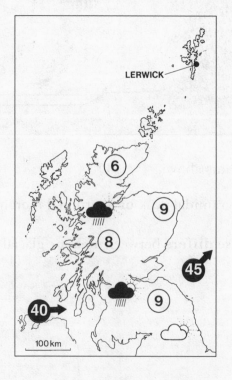

3. (continued)

Reference Diagram Q3C: Air Pressure
Wednesday 6 November 1996 (Lerwick)

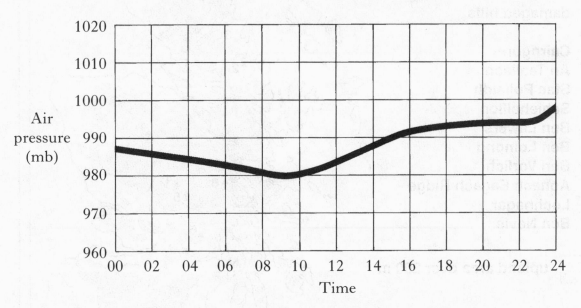

Reference Diagram Q3D: Anemometer Graph for
Wednesday 6 November 1996 (Lerwick)

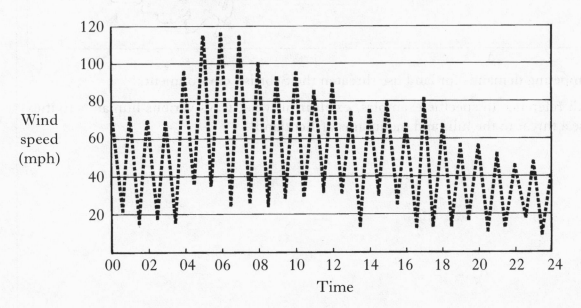

Look at Reference Diagrams Q3A, Q3B, Q3C and Q3D.

Explain the relationships between air pressure and other weather elements during Wednesday 6 November.

6

[Turn over

4.   **Reference Diagram Q4: Scotland's 10 Most Damaged Hills**

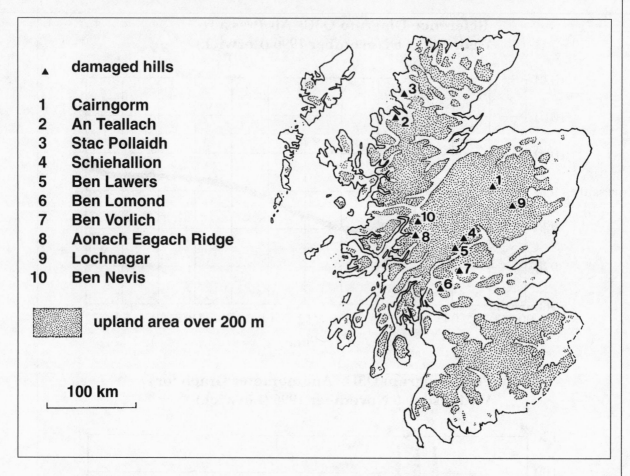

▲   **damaged hills**

1	**Cairngorm**
2	**An Teallach**
3	**Stac Pollaidh**
4	**Schiehallion**
5	**Ben Lawers**
6	**Ben Lomond**
7	**Ben Vorlich**
8	**Aonach Eagach Ridge**
9	**Lochnagar**
10	**Ben Nevis**

upland area over 200 m

100 km

Competing demands for land use threaten the Scottish environment.

With reference to specific examples, **explain** in what ways various human activities pose a threat to the hills and mountains of Scotland.

     4

5. Reference Diagram Q5: The Distribution of the Chemical Industry in Germany

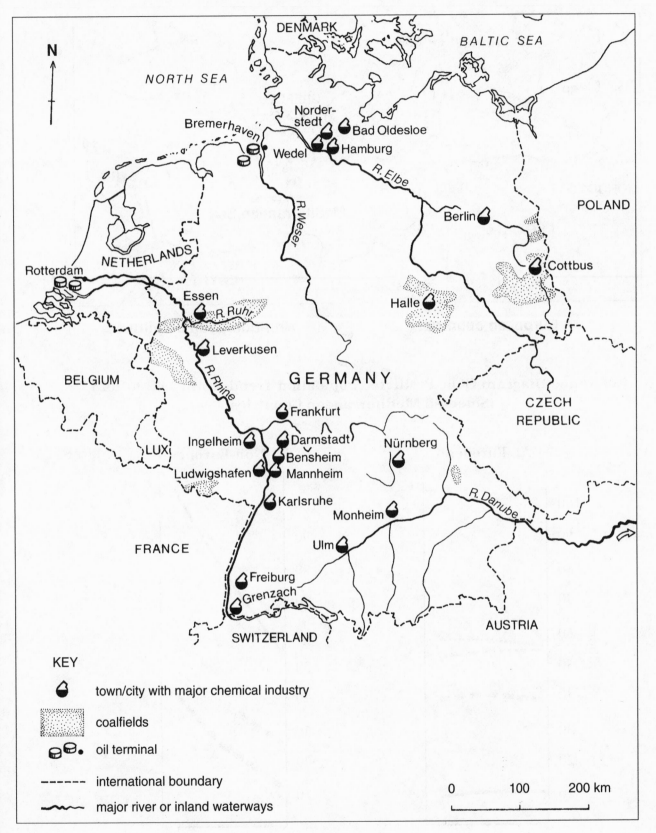

KEY

△ town/city with major chemical industry

▒ coalfields

⬤🛢• oil terminal

------ international boundary

～～ major river or inland waterways

0   100   200 km

	Marks	
	KU	EV

Explain the location of chemical works in Germany.   6

6.   **Reference Diagram Q6A: Selected Countries of the Mediterranean**

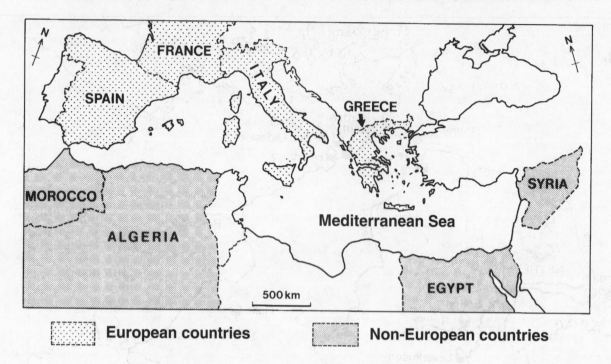

European countries   Non-European countries

Reference Diagram Q6B: Predicted Population Trends from 1991 to 2025
(Selected Mediterranean Countries)

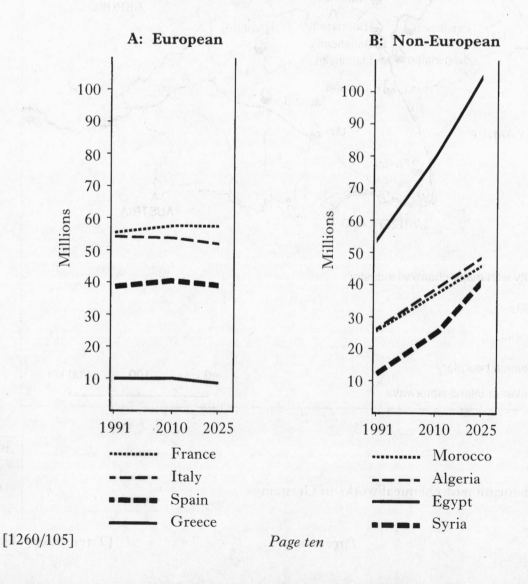

A: European   B: Non-European

.... France   .... Morocco
– – – Italy   – – – Algeria
■■■■ Spain   ——— Egypt
——— Greece   ■■■■ Syria

Marks
| | KU | EV |

6. (continued)

Study Reference Diagrams Q6A and Q6B.

(*a*) Compare **in detail** the population changes predicted for the European countries with those changes predicted for the non-European countries.

4

(*b*) Choose one European **and** one non-European country in the Mediterranean region.

For each of your chosen countries, suggest measures that their governments should be taking in response to the predicted population changes.

5

[Turn over

7.   **Reference Diagram Q7A: Selected Countries of West Africa**

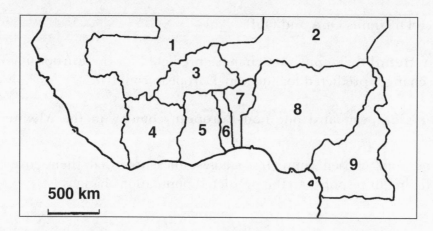

500 km

Key	1	Mali	4	Ivory Coast	7	Benin
	2	Niger	5	Ghana	8	Nigeria
	3	Burkina	6	Togo	9	Cameroon

Reference Diagram Q7B: Percentage of females aged 5–15 enrolled in school

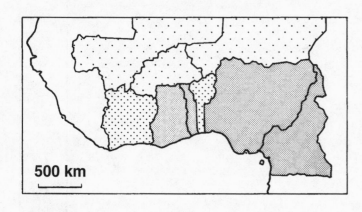

500 km

Reference Diagram Q7C: Percentage of males aged 5–15 enrolled in school

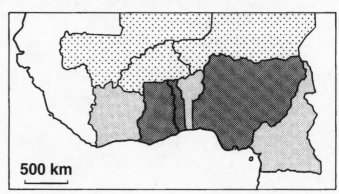

500 km

KEY

■ 60–79%   ▦ 40–59%   ⬚ 20–39%   □ less than 20%

Look at Reference Diagrams Q7A, Q7B and Q7C.

(a) Compare the general pattern of school enrolment for males and females in West Africa.

(b) Suggest what problems this pattern could create for the future development of West Africa.

4

Marks

KU | EV

8. **Reference Diagram Q8A: World Map drawn in Proportion to GNP of Countries**

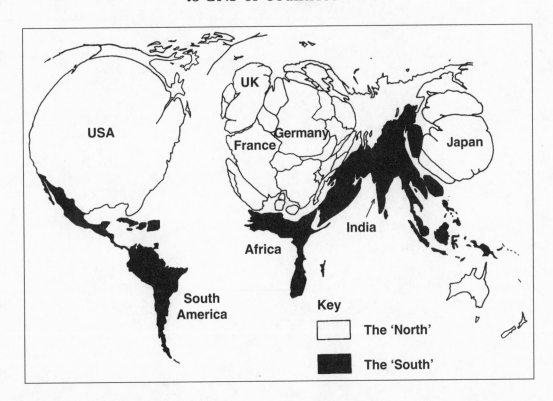

Reference Diagram Q8B: Location of the World's 50 Largest Companies

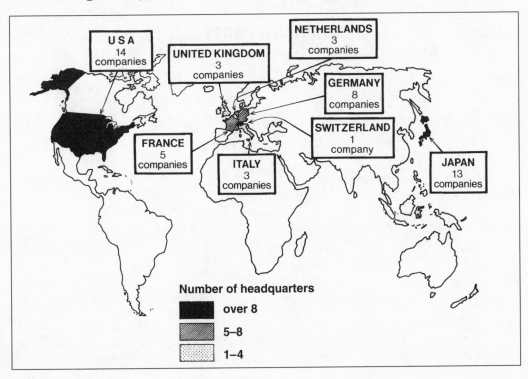

Look at Reference Diagrams Q8A and Q8B above.

(a) **Describe**, **in detail**, the distribution of world wealth shown in Reference Diagram Q8A.

3

(b) **Explain** the distribution of the world's largest companies shown in Reference Diagram Q8B.

4

[END OF QUESTION PAPER]

[BLANK PAGE]

[BLANK PAGE]

[BLANK PAGE]

C

1260/105

SCOTTISH
CERTIFICATE OF
EDUCATION
1999

TUESDAY, 11 MAY
10.45 AM – 12.45 PM

GEOGRAPHY
STANDARD GRADE
Credit Level

All questions should be attempted.

Candidates should read the questions carefully. Answers should be clearly expressed and relevant.

Credit will always be given for appropriate sketch-maps and diagrams.

Write legibly and neatly, and leave a space of about one cm between the lines.

Marks may be deducted for bad spelling and bad punctuation, and for writing that is difficult to read.

All maps and diagrams in this paper have been printed in black only: no other colours have been used.

SCOTTISH
QUALIFICATIONS
AUTHORITY

1:50 000 Scale
Landranger Series

Four colours should appear above; if not then please return to the invigilator.
Four colours should appear above; if not then please return to the invigilator.

Extract No 1138/90

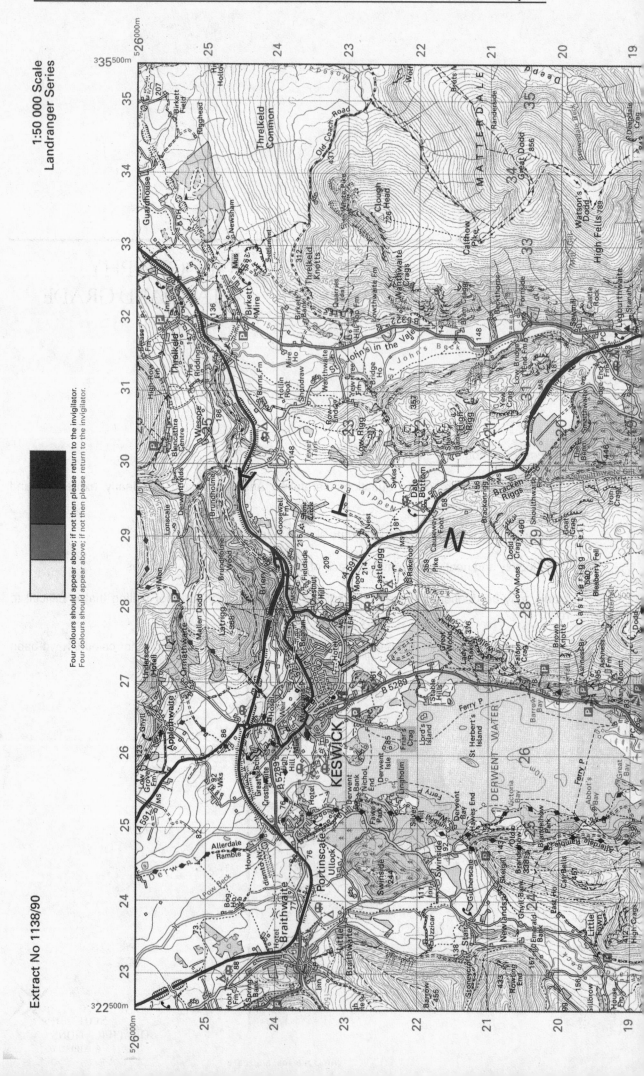

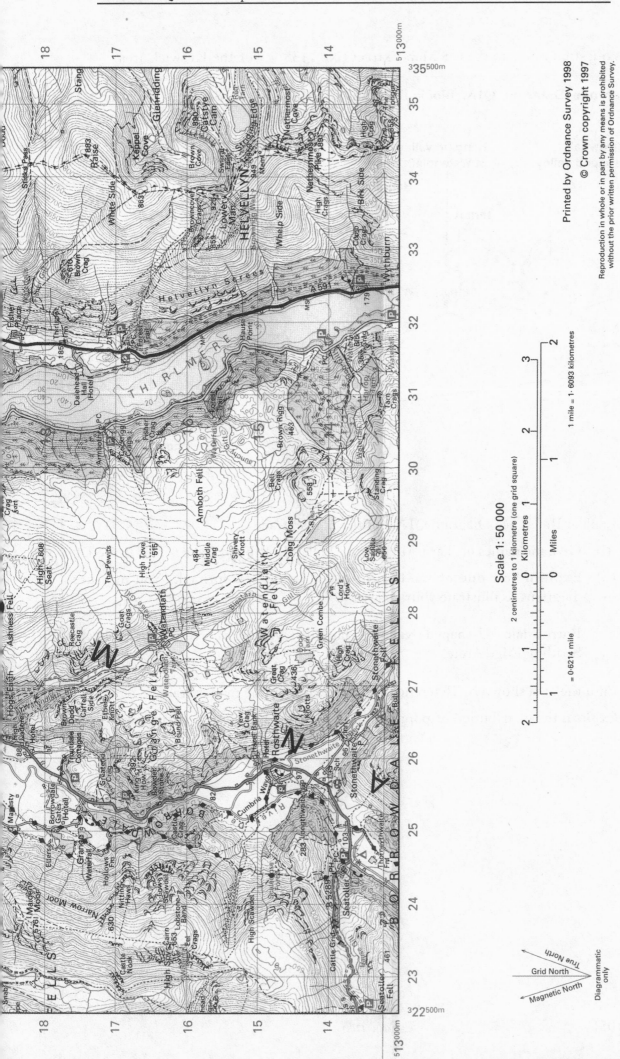

Scale 1: 50 000

2 centimetres to 1 kilometre (one grid square)

Printed by Ordnance Survey 1998

© Crown copyright 1997

Reproduction in whole or in part by any means is prohibited
without the prior written permission of Ordnance Survey.

Map reproduced from Ordnance Survey mapping with the permission of the
Controller of Her Majesty's Stationery Office, © Crown copyright, Licence No. 100036009.

True North
Grid North
Magnetic North
Diagrammatic
only

1. This question refers to the OS Map Extract (No 1138/90) of the Keswick area.

Reference Diagram Q1A: Block Diagram of Map Extract South of Northing 17

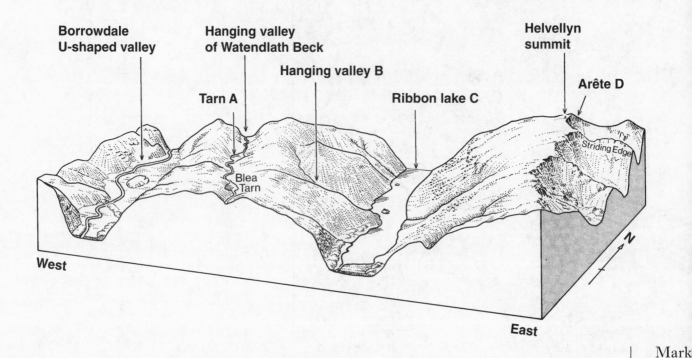

<table>
<tr><td></td><td>Mark</td></tr>
<tr><td></td><td>KU</td></tr>
</table>

(*a*) Look at Reference Diagram Q1A and the map extract.

   (i) Give the names of Tarn A, Hanging Valley B, Ribbon Lake C and Arête D.   **3**

   (ii) **Explain** how **one** of the features listed below was formed. You may use diagrams to illustrate your answer.

      Borrowdale U-shaped valley, Hanging Valley of Watendlath Beck, Striding Edge Arête.   **4**

(*b*) Find the area shown by Reference Diagram Q1B on the map extract.

   Explain the distribution of population as indicated by the settlement map.

1. (continued)

Reference Diagram Q1B: Distribution of Settlement

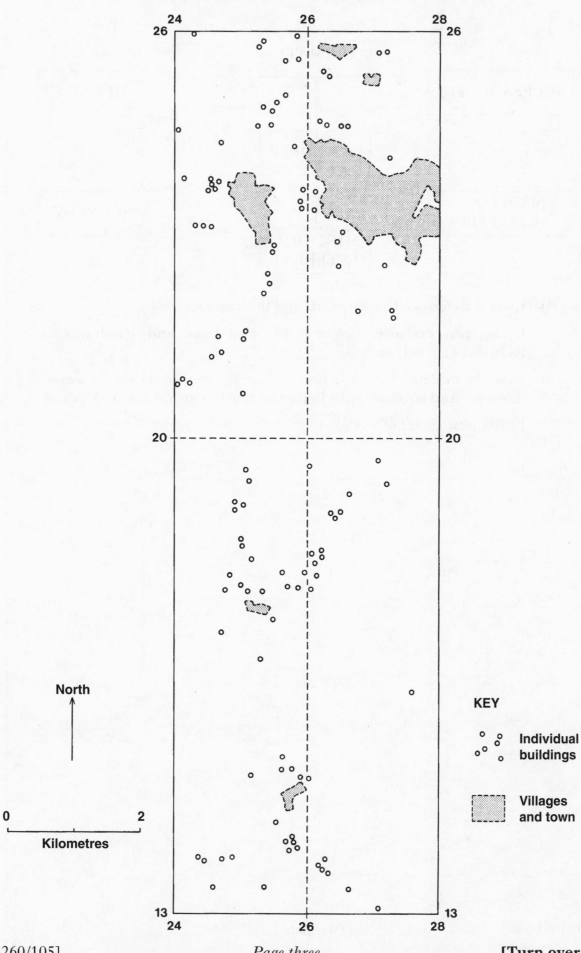

1. (continued)

Reference Diagram Q1C: Factors influencing Tourism

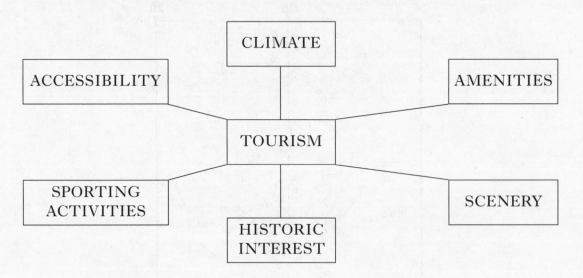

(c) (i)   Look at Reference Diagram Q1C and the map extract.

Using map evidence, describe the advantages **and** disadvantages of Keswick as a holiday resort.

(ii) Describe in detail two gathering techniques you would use to assess the economic **and** environmental impact of tourism in and around Keswick.

Justify your choice of techniques.

Marks

KU	ES

2.   **Reference Diagram Q2: Field Sketch of the Upper Course of a Valley**

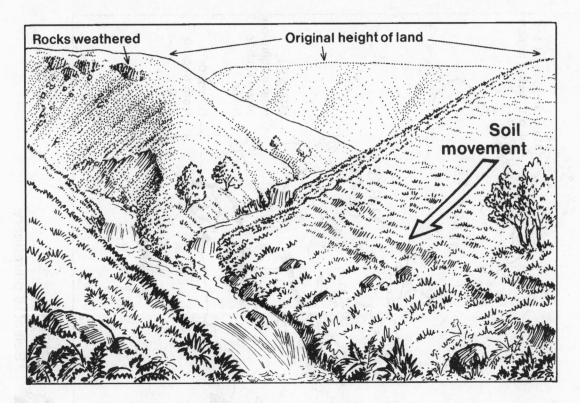

Look at the Reference Diagram Q2 above.

Explain how the V-shaped valley was formed.   4

[Turn over

3.

Reference Diagram Q3A: Pollution in the Mediterranean

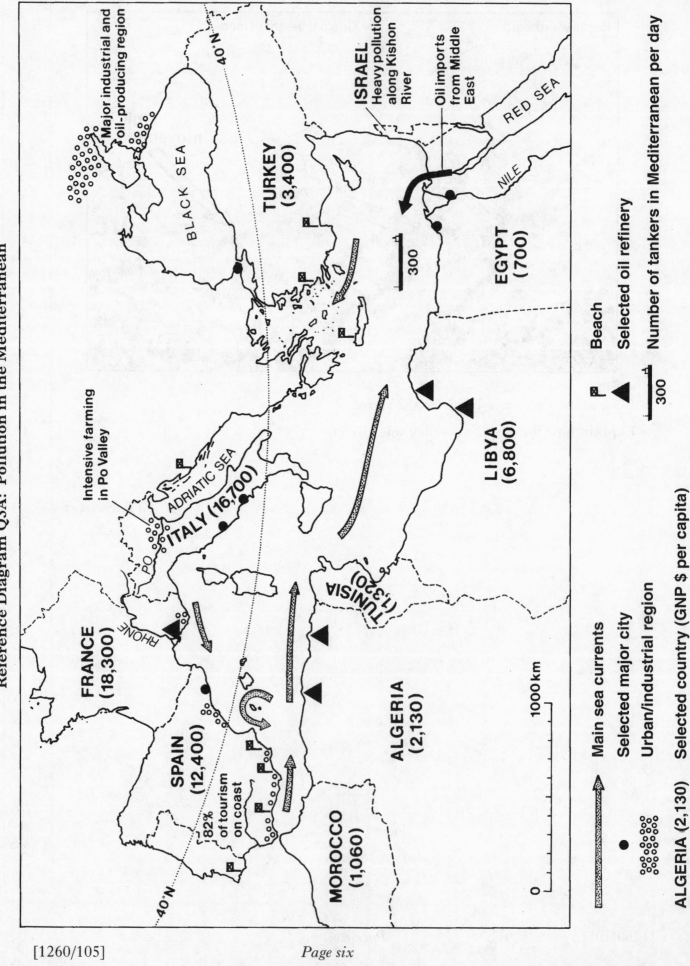

Marks	
KU	ES

3. (continued)

Reference Diagram Q3B: Expected Population Growth of the Mediterranean Coastal Regions

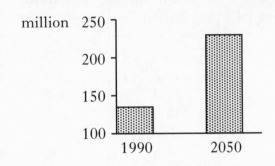

Reference Diagram Q3C: Sources of Pollution in the Mediterranean

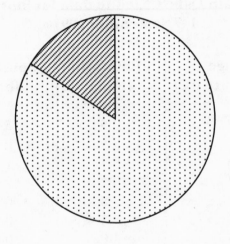

 pollution originating from activities on land

pollution originating from activities at sea

Look at Reference Diagrams Q3A, Q3B and Q3C.

(a) **Explain** why the Mediterranean Sea suffers from severe pollution.   6

(b) "Solving the Mediterranean's pollution problem requires international cooperation. We have a common interest. All Mediterranean countries, rich and poor, will have to make sacrifices to clean up and protect the Mediterranean. Penalties for chemical pollution must be tough!"

(Spokesperson for Environmental Organisation)

What are the arguments for **and** against accepting the proposals to solve the Mediterranean's pollution problem?   4

[Turn over

4.   **Reference Diagram Q4A: Climatic Data for Glasgow Airport**
                                1–7 September 1997

Date	Average Temperature (°C)	Rainfall (mm)	Sunshine (hrs)	Wind Direction
1	14·4	0·9	3·7	W
2	12·1	12·6	1·0	S
3	16·8	11·3	1·7	S
4	14·5	10·4	8·3	SW
5	14·7	Trace	4·1	SW
6	13·5	1·6	4·0	SW
7	15·1	0·4	0·0	W

Reference Diagram Q4B: Climatic data for Stornoway Airport
                          1–7 September 1997

Date	Average Temperature (°C)	Rainfall (mm)	Sunshine (hrs)	Wind Direction
1	15·2	0·9	5·0	NW
2	13·2	3·9	0·8	S
3	13·6	8·4	1·1	S
4	12·4	19·1	2·6	S
5	12·0	7·8	0·1	W
6	12·4	5·5	0·4	W
7	13·3	3·8	0·0	SW

Look at Reference Diagrams Q4A and Q4B.

Which processing techniques would you use to **compare** the statistics for the two airports?

Justify your choice of techniques.

5.   **Reference Diagram Q5: Oykell Farm in the Northwest Highlands**

Look at Reference Diagram Q5.

Oykell Farm experiences a number of difficulties due to the climate, the type of land
and its location in the Northwest Highlands.

Explain the decisions which the farmer could take to overcome these difficulties and
to ensure a reasonable income from the farm.

You must refer to both farming **and** non-farming activities.

6.   **Reference Diagram Q6A: Location of an Asian Electronics**
Semi-conductor Factory

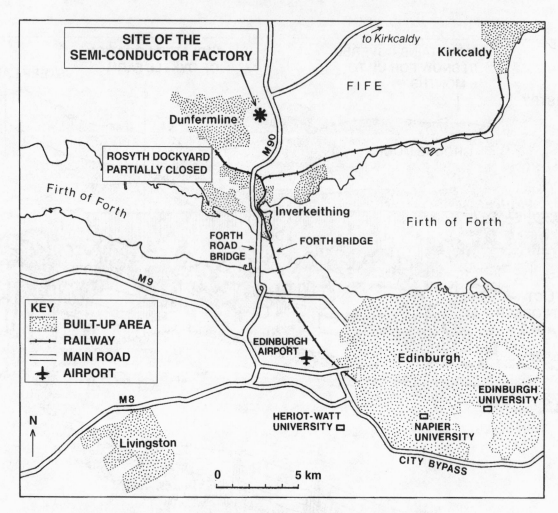

Reference Diagram Q6B: The Asian Semi-conductor Factory, Fife

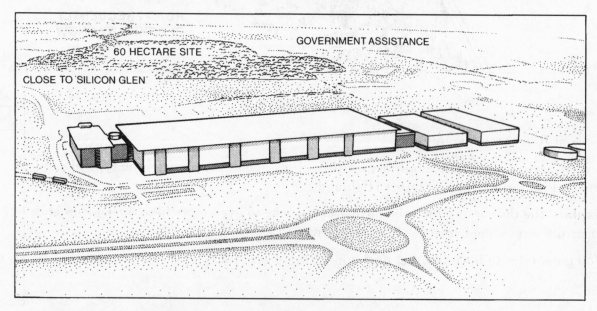

Study Reference Diagrams Q6A and Q6B.

In 1997, an Asian electronics company built a new factory near Dunfermline to produce computer chips (semi-conductors).

Explain the advantages of this site and its location in Fife **for** the company.   6

7.   **Reference Diagram Q7A: Percentage Growth of World Trade Share for Selected Countries 1980–1992**

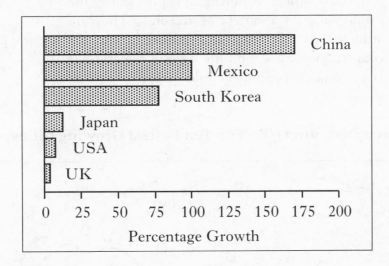

Reference Table Q7B: Selected Statistics for China, Japan and USA 1992

	China	**Japan**	**USA**
Land area (sq km)	9 596 960	377 800	9 809 431
Population (million)	1185	125	264
World trade figures (million US dollars)	165 000	572 000	1 000 000
Literacy (percentage)	70	99	99
Labour Costs (US dollars per hour)	1	16·5	16

Look at Reference Diagram Q7A and Reference Table Q7B.

"Japan and USA are currently dominant in international relations and trade. However, by the year 2020, China will have overtaken both Japan and USA."

Do you agree with this statement? Give reasons for your answer.   5

[Turn over

Mark

KU

8.   **Reference Text Q8A**

> "In Developing countries people leave the
> countryside for a variety of reasons. They are
> attracted by the city and pushed from the
> countryside. Most find life hard in the city but
> large numbers continue to move there."

Reference Diagram Q8B: The Ten Fastest Growing Cities

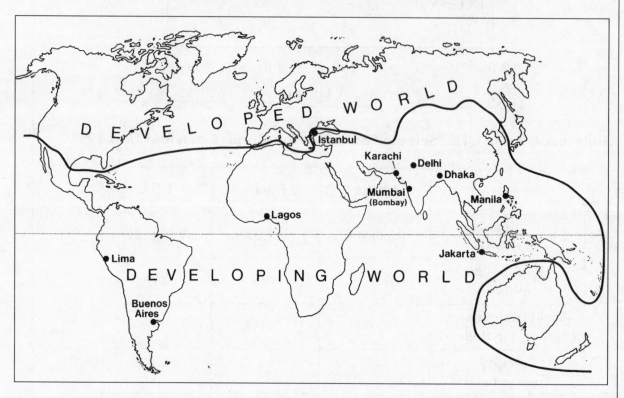

Reference Text Q8C: Problems of Fast Growing Cities in the Developing Countries

> Higher living costs
>
> Not enough formal jobs
>
> Shortage of good housing
>
> Pollution and overcrowding

8. (continued)

Study Reference Texts Q8A and Q8C and Reference Diagram Q8B.

(a) Despite the problems outlined in Reference Text Q8C, large numbers of people in **Developing** Countries are still moving from the countryside to the cities. **Explain** why this is happening.

6

(b) In **Developed** countries the population in many large cities such as Chicago and London is static or falling.

Give reasons for this.

4

[Turn over

Mark

KU

9.   **Reference Diagram Q9: Two Approaches to Development in India**

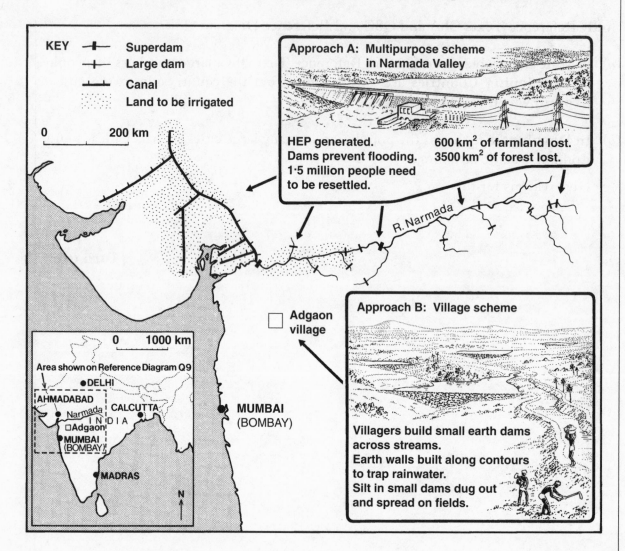

Look at Reference Diagram Q9 above.

The problem in this part of India is that there is a dry season and unpredictable rainfall.

Which approach, **A** or **B**, do you think is the more appropriate for a Developing Country such as India?

Give reasons for your answer.

10.   **Reference Diagram Q10A: Possible Effects of giving Aid to Developing Countries**

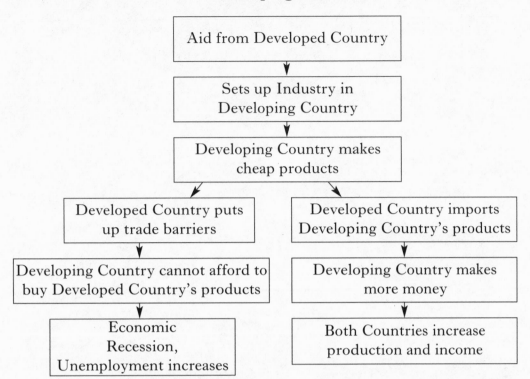

```
        Aid from Developed Country
                    │
                    ▼
        Sets up Industry in
        Developing Country
                    │
                    ▼
        Developing Country makes
        cheap products
              ↙           ↘
Developed Country puts     Developed Country imports
up trade barriers          Developing Country's products
        │                           │
        ▼                           ▼
Developing Country cannot afford to   Developing Country makes
buy Developed Country's products      more money
        │                           │
        ▼                           ▼
    Economic                    Both Countries increase
    Recession,                  production and income
Unemployment increases
```

Reference Diagram Q10B: Percentage of GNP spent on Aid by Developed Countries

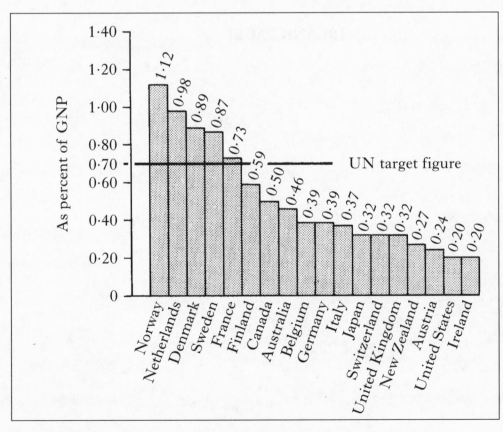

Look at Reference Diagrams Q10A and Q10B.

"Developed Countries are keen to give aid to Developing Countries because of the benefits involved."

Do you agree with this statement? Give reasons for your answer.   4

[END OF QUESTION PAPER]

[BLANK PAGE]

C

1260/405

NATIONAL QUALIFICATIONS 2000	MONDAY, 5 JUNE 10.45 AM – 12.45 PM	GEOGRAPHY STANDARD GRADE Credit Level

All questions should be attempted.

Candidates should read the questions carefully. Answers should be clearly expressed and relevant.

Credit will always be given for appropriate sketch-maps and diagrams.

Write legibly and neatly, and leave a space of about one cm between the lines.

Marks may be deducted for bad spelling and bad punctuation, and for writing that is difficult to read.

All maps and diagrams in this paper have been printed in black only: no other colours have been used.

SCOTTISH QUALIFICATIONS AUTHORITY

Extract No 1173/93

1:50 000 Scale
Landranger Series

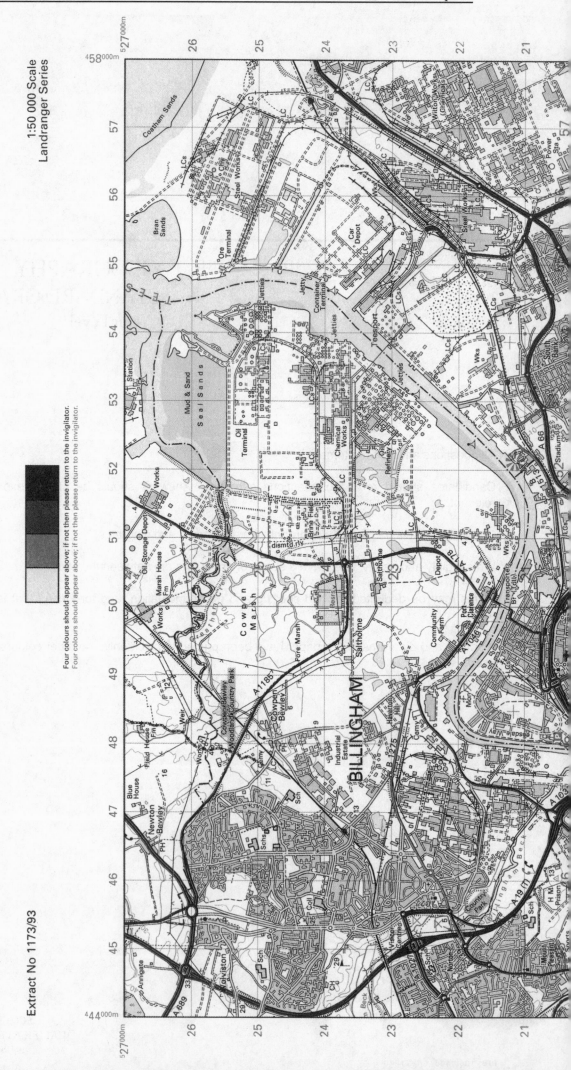

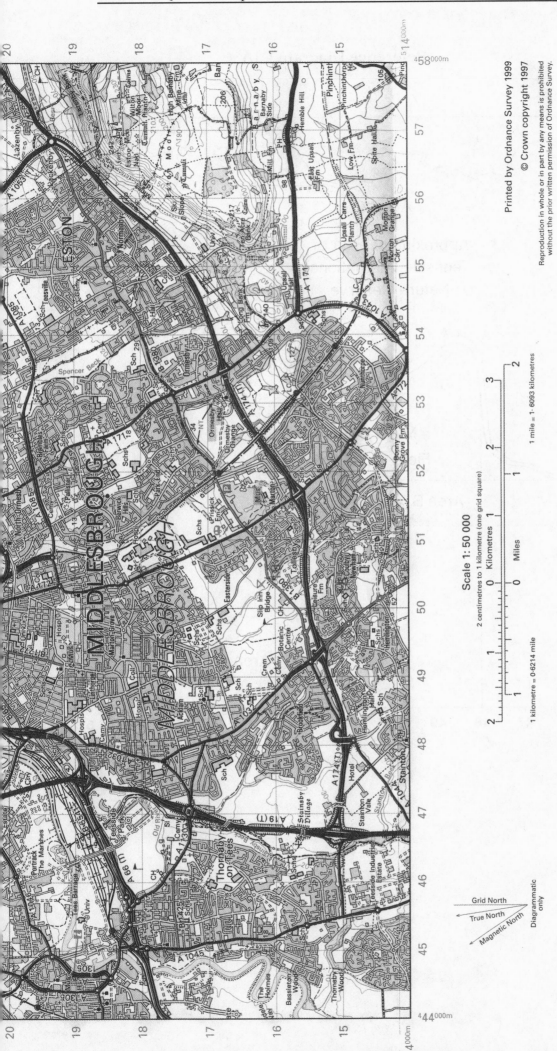

Scale 1: 50 000

2 centimetres to 1 kilometre (one grid square)

1 kilometre = 0·6214 mile

1 mile = 1·6093 kilometres

Grid North

True North

Magnetic North

Diagrammatic
only

1.   **Reference Diagram Q1A**

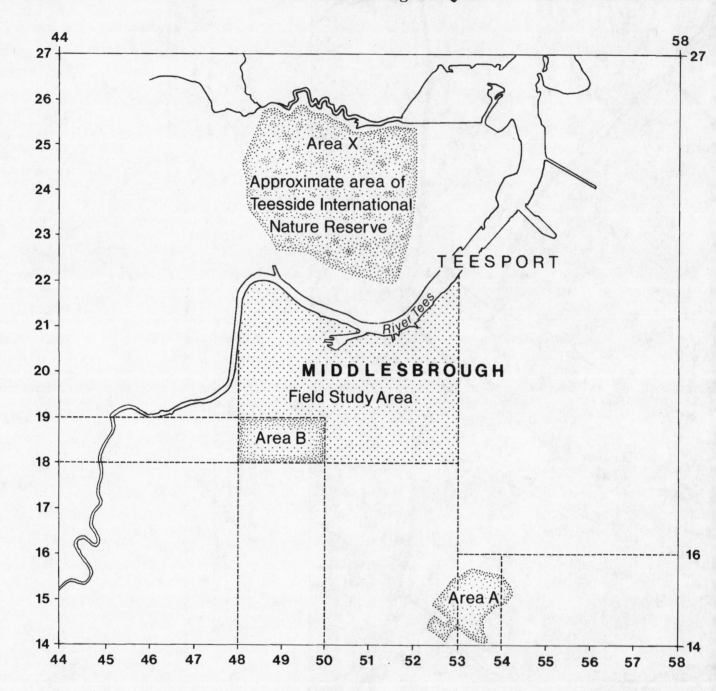

Marks
| KU | ES |

1. (continued)

This question refers to the OS Map Extract (No 1173/93) of the Middlesbrough area and Reference Diagram Q1A.

(a) Give the four figure grid reference of the square which contains Middlesbrough's CBD (Central Business District). Give reasons for your answer.

3

(b) A group of students has been asked to gather information about urban and industrial change in the field study area marked on Reference Diagram Q1A.

Describe in detail the gathering techniques they might use to complete such an assignment. Justify your choices.

5

(c) Describe the differences between the two urban environments of Nunthorpe (Area A) and Linthorpe/Marton Grove (Area B), labelled on Reference Diagram Q1A.

5

(d) **Reference Diagram Q1B: Location of Middlesbrough/Teesport**

Teesport is one of Britain's largest ports and is the second largest petrochemicals port in Europe.

Using **map evidence** as well as Reference Diagram Q1B, **explain** the advantages of site and situation which Teesport has for manufacturing industries such as petrochemicals.

6

1. (continued)

(e) Describe the **physical** features of the River Tees **and** its valley from Basselton Wood (446157) to the road bridge at (475194).

4

(f)   **Reference Text Q1C: Teesside International Nature Reserve**

Area:	1000 hectares
Investment:	£11 million between 1998 and 2008
Managed by:	Teesside Environment Trust
Proposal:	Creation of a massive open water, reedbed and swamp system. Construction of a visitor centre, bird hides and a system of board walks through existing mudflats, salt marsh and open grassland.
Wildlife:	Includes endangered wading birds such as snipe, redshank, bittern and other migratory species.

Look at Reference Text Q1C and Reference Diagram Q1A and locate Area X on the Ordnance Survey map.

Give the advantages **and** disadvantages of this site for a nature reserve.

2.   **Reference Diagram Q2: Weather Conditions over British Isles**
                                October 1998

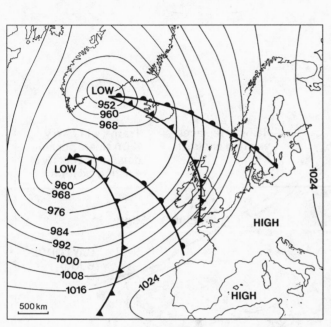

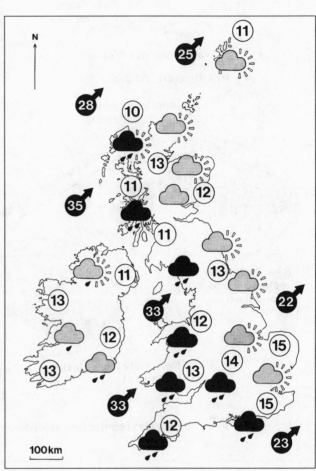

	Marks	
	KU	ES

Look at Reference Diagram Q2.

Explain the differences in weather between the East and West of the British Isles.   6

[Turn over

3.   Reference Diagram Q3A: The Cairn Gorm Mountain Railway

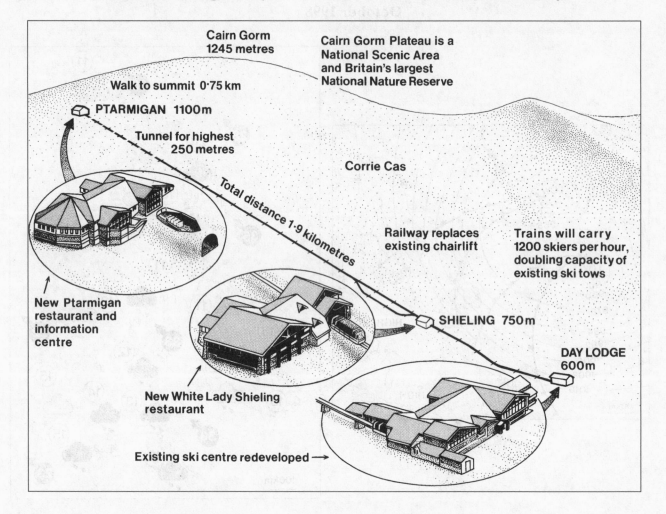

Cairn Gorm
1245 metres

Cairn Gorm Plateau is a
National Scenic Area
and Britain's largest
National Nature Reserve

Walk to summit 0·75 km

PTARMIGAN 1100m

Tunnel for highest
250 metres

Corrie Cas

Total distance 1·9 kilometres

Railway replaces
existing chairlift

Trains will carry
1200 skiers per hour,
doubling capacity of
existing ski tows

New Ptarmigan
restaurant and
information
centre

SHIELING 750m

DAY LODGE
600m

New White Lady Shieling
restaurant

Existing ski centre redeveloped →

Reference Diagram Q3B: Area around Aviemore and the Cairngorms

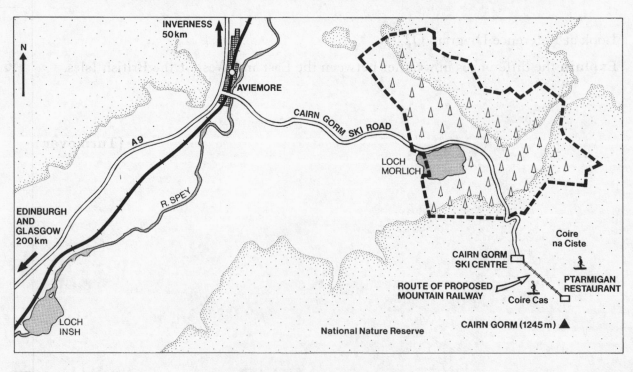

INVERNESS
50 km

N

AVIEMORE

CAIRN GORM SKI ROAD

A9

LOCH
MORLICH

R. SPEY

EDINBURGH
AND
GLASGOW
200 km

Coire
na Ciste

CAIRN GORM
SKI CENTRE

PTARMIGAN
RESTAURANT

ROUTE OF PROPOSED
MOUNTAIN RAILWAY

Coire Cas

LOCH
INSH

National Nature Reserve

CAIRN GORM (1245 m) ▲

KEY

Land over
400 Metres

Glenmore
Forest Park

Ski slopes

Scale 1 km

3. (continued)

Reference Table Q3C: Selected Statistics for Aviemore and the Cairngorms

	With existing Ski Tows and Chairlifts	Estimated Figures after Opening of Mountain Railway
Cairn Gorm Ski Centre income	£3 million	£5 million
% of total income earned in winter months	90	50
People travelling up to Ptarmigan Restaurant in summer	55 000	125 000
People walking from Ptarmigan to Cairn Gorm summit in summer	4400	12 500
Tourist related jobs in Aviemore area	600	960

Marks

	KU	ES

(a)   Study Reference Diagrams Q3A and Q3B and Reference Table Q3C.

"This development will be of tremendous benefit to the area."

Do you agree with this statement about the Cairn Gorm Mountain Railway? Give detailed reasons for your answer.   **6**

(b)   University students will carry out a survey to assess the possible impact of the Cairn Gorm Mountain Railway on the area.

Which gathering techniques might they use to obtain appropriate data?

Explain in detail your choice of techniques.   **5**

[Turn over

4.

Reference Text Q4A: Eire in the 1950s

> In the 1950s, Eire was a country based on agriculture and characterised by emigration and a fairly low standard of living.

Reference Diagram Q4B: Location of Eire in the EU

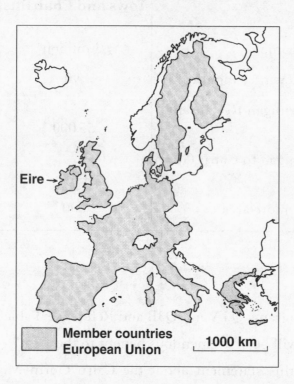

Reference Diagram Q4C: Eire in the late 1990s

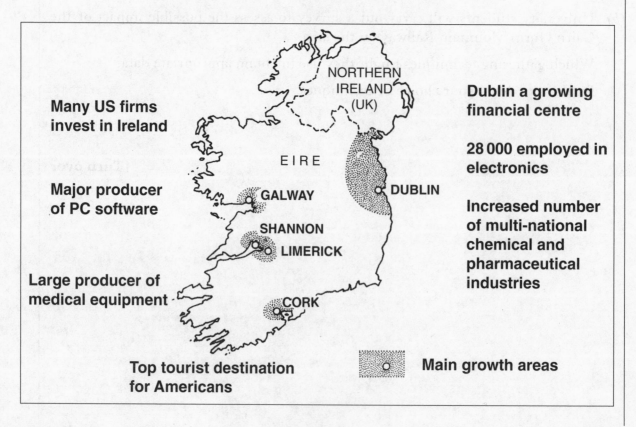

Marks

KU	ES

4. (continued)

Reference Text Q4D: Why firms are going to Eire

> • Labour costs low by EU Standards
>
> • Many university graduates
>
> • Favourable tax system
>
> • High quality environment

Study Reference Text Q4A, Reference Diagrams Q4B and Q4C and Reference Text Q4D.

"Over the last thirty years the economy of Eire has changed as many foreign firms have chosen to locate there."

Describe in detail the advantages **and** disadvantages which economic change has brought to Eire.

6

[Turn over

5.   **Reference Diagram Q5: Oil Industry in the Niger Delta (West Africa)**

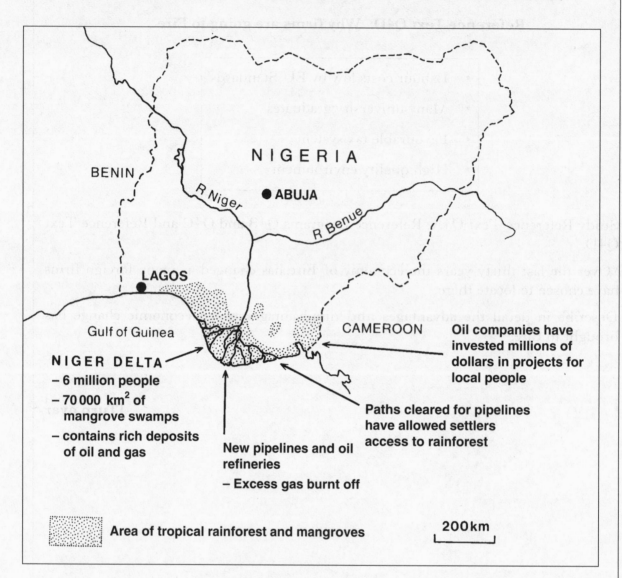

Reference Table Q5: Facts about Oil in the Niger Delta

% of Nigeria's exports provided by oil	90
Number of oil spills in the Niger Delta (1976–1991)	2976
Number of people employed in the oil industry in Nigeria	25 000

Study Reference Diagram Q5 and Reference Table Q5.

"The damage caused to the rainforest environment in the Niger Delta is a small price to pay for the huge benefits which the oil industry has brought to the people of the area."

Do you agree with this statement? Give reasons for your answer.

6. **Reference Diagram Q6A: Selected Statistics on International Debt**

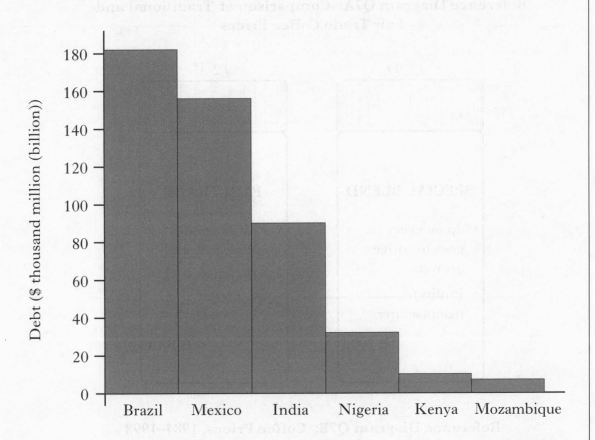

Reference Text Q6B

"Jubilee 2000 is encouraging Governments and International Banks to cancel the debts of many of the world's poorest countries."

Study Reference Diagram Q6A and Reference Text Q6B.

Explain how debt causes major problems for many developing countries.

4

[Turn over

7.   **Reference Diagram Q7A: Comparison of Traditional and
                        Fair Trade Coffee Prices**

£1·99   £2·35

SPECIAL BLEND   **FAIR TRADE**

• 2p on every jar   • Profits go to
  goes to coffee   coffee grower
  grower
                                           • Minimum price
• Profits to   for grower
  manufacturer   guaranteed

              e 100 g   e 100 g

**Reference Diagram Q7B: Coffee Prices, 1984–1998
                    (Coffee Beans)**

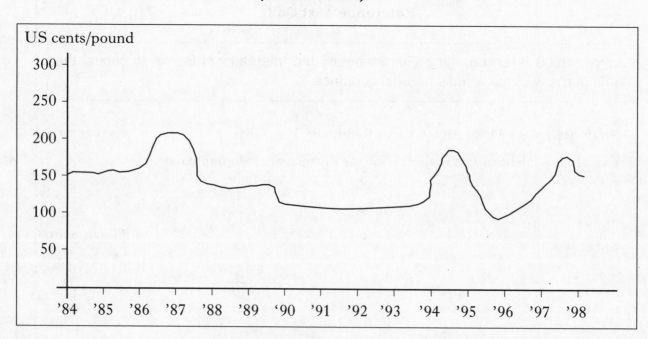

7. (continued)

Reference Text Q7C: Extract from Fair Trade Advertisement

Perfect Coffee and How to Make It

- Warm the pot, add one heaped spoon of freshly roasted Fair Trade coffee.

- Filter out the middleman.

- Provide coffee farmers with a regular income.

- Help turn mud and straw houses into bricks and mortar.

- Enjoy your coffee . . . and help build a brighter future for the next generation.

- A better deal guaranteed for coffee growers.

Look at Reference Diagrams Q7A and Q7B and Reference Text Q7C.

Explain how the idea of Fair Trade is a way of helping coffee growers in the Developing World.

4

[Turn over

8.   **Reference Table Q8: Selected Data for 5 Countries**

	Land Area (sq km)	Population (million)	GDP ($/head)	Exports ($ million)	Imports ($ million)	Urban (percent)
USA	9 100 000	255	22 470	428	499	75
Brazil	8 400 000	150	2300	31	21	74
Japan	374 000	124	19 000	314	236	77
India	2 900 000	882	380	20	25	25
Russia	17 000 000	149	2240	58	43	74

Look at Reference Table Q8.

(*a*) Suggest **two** methods you could use to show **relationships** between different data in the table. Justify your choices in detail.

(*b*) "Population size and land area are the main indicators which show the international importance of a country."

Do you agree with the above statement? Give reasons for your answer.

9.   **Reference Diagram Q9A: Population Density of Peru**

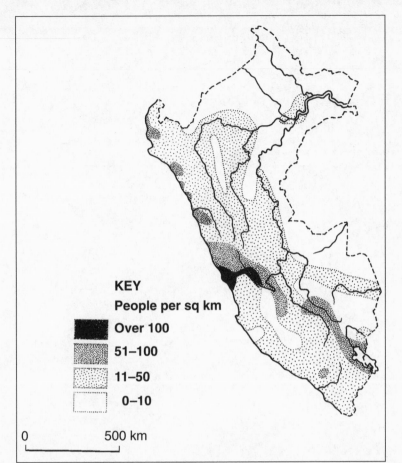

KEY

People per sq km

■ Over 100

▨ 51–100

░ 11–50

· 0–10

0   500 km

Reference Diagram Q9B:
Resources and Industry of Peru

Reference Diagram Q9C:
Physical Features of Peru

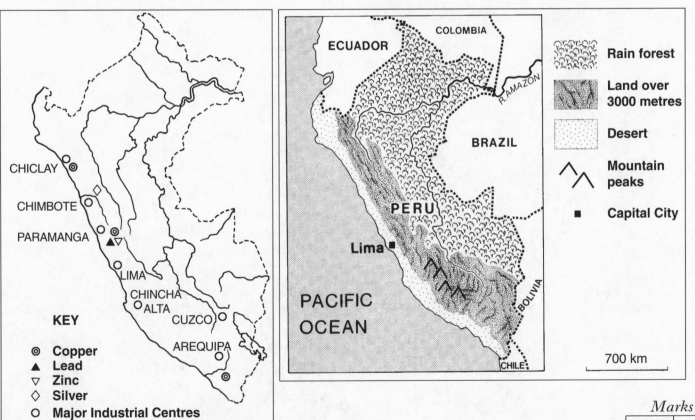

KEY

◎ Copper
▲ Lead
▽ Zinc
◇ Silver
○ Major Industrial Centres

Look at Reference Diagrams Q9A, Q9B and Q9C above.

Explain the population distribution of Peru.

[END OF QUESTION PAPER]

Marks

KU | ES

4

[BLANK PAGE]

C

1260/405

NATIONAL
QUALIFICATIONS
2001

WEDNESDAY, 23 MAY
10.45 AM – 12.45 PM

GEOGRAPHY
STANDARD GRADE
Credit Level

All questions should be attempted.

Candidates should read the questions carefully. Answers should be clearly expressed and relevant.

Credit will always be given for appropriate sketch-maps and diagrams.

Write legibly and neatly, and leave a space of about one cm between the lines.

Marks may be deducted for bad spelling and bad punctuation, and for writing that is difficult to read.

All maps and diagrams in this paper have been printed in black only: no other colours have been used.

SCOTTISH
QUALIFICATIONS
AUTHORITY

1:50 000 Scale
Landranger Series

Four colours should appear above; if not then please return to the invigilator.
Four colours should appear above; if not then please return to the invigilator.

Extract No 1213/19/24/25

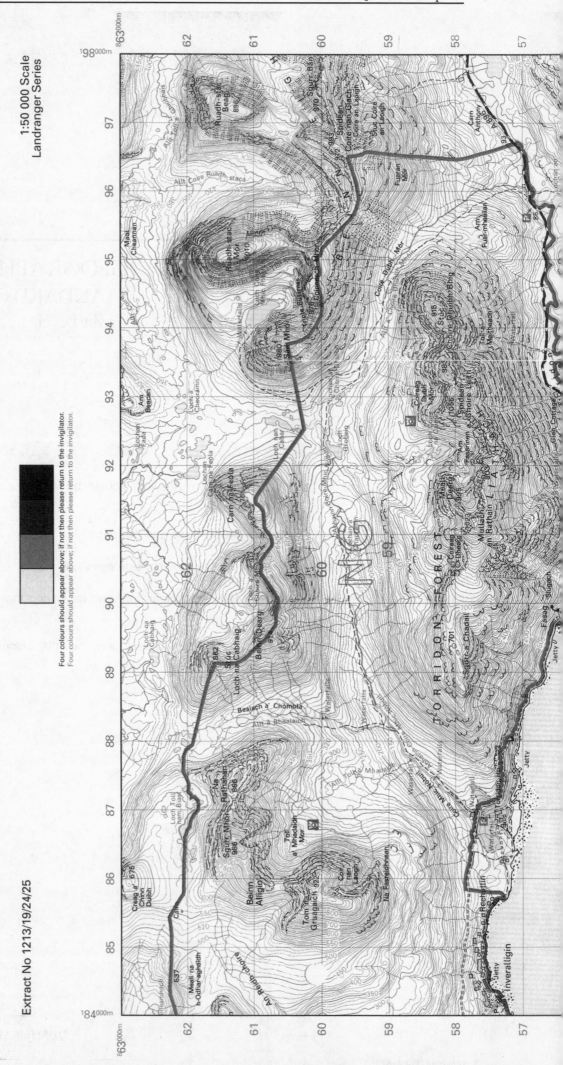

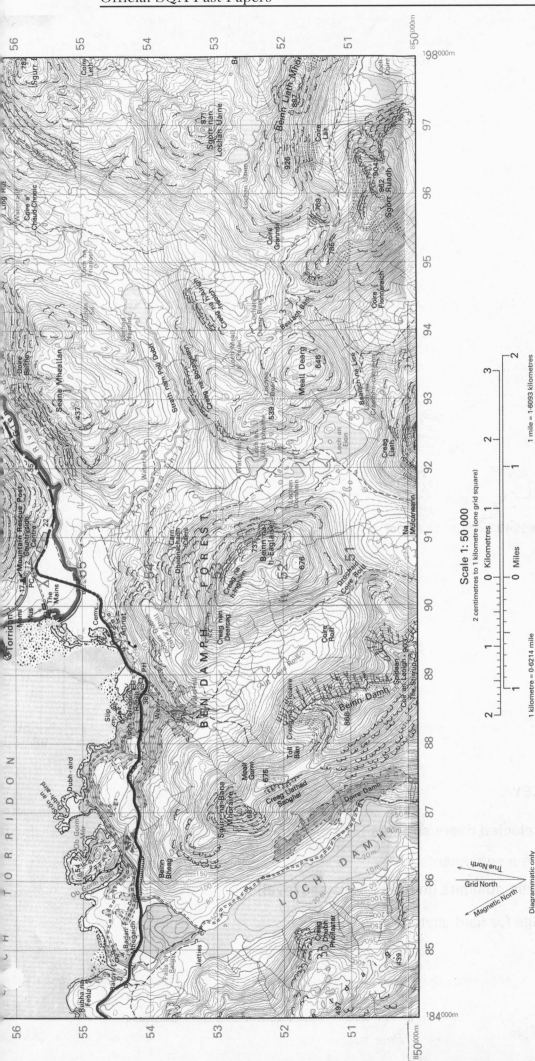

Scale 1: 50 000

2 centimetres to 1 kilometre (one grid square)

1 kilometre = 0·6214 mile   1 mile = 1·6093 kilometres

Grid North

True North

Magnetic North

Diagrammatic only

Map reproduced from Ordnance Survey mapping with the permission of the
Controller of Her Majesty's Stationery Office, © Crown copyright, Licence No. 100036009.

1.   **Reference Diagram Q1A**

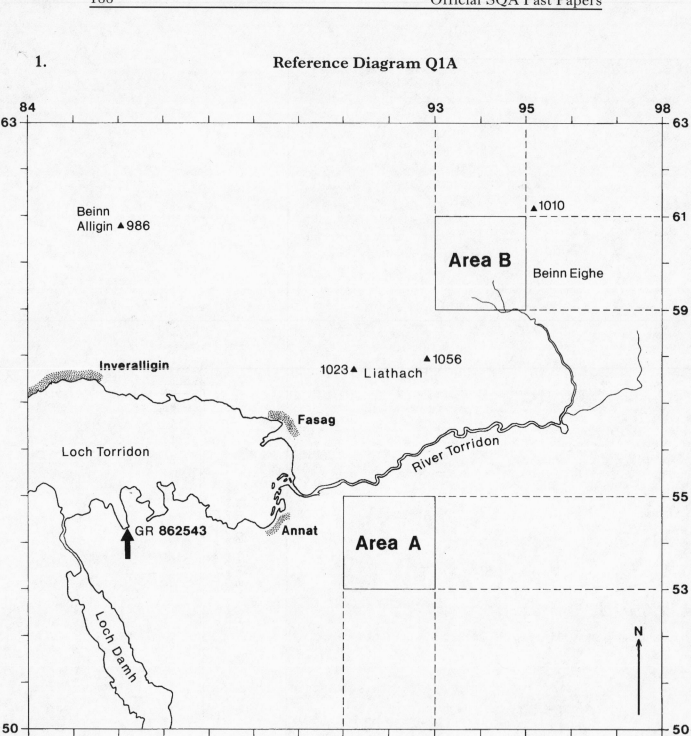

KEY

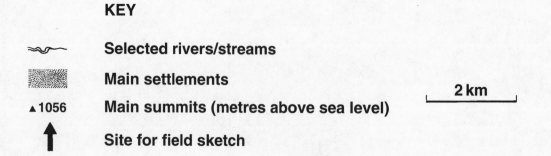

Selected rivers/streams
Main settlements
▲1056 Main summits (metres above sea level)
Site for field sketch

2 km

1. (continued)

This question refers to the OS Map Extract (No 1213/19/24/25) of Torridon and Reference Diagram Q1A on *Page two*.

(*a*) The area covered by the map extract is one of Scotland's most spectacular mountain landscapes.

   (i) Match each of the features named below with the correct grid reference.

     Features: pyramidal peak,   hanging valley,   arete,   corrie

     Choose from:

     Grid references: 952588,   923580,   852585,   860601,   925576   **3**

   (ii) **Explain** how **one** of the features listed in (*a*)(i) was formed. You may use diagrams to illustrate your answer.   **4**

(*b*) Look at Reference Diagram Q1A.

A commercial forestry company surveyed the map area's potential for forestry. It considered Area A to be more suitable than Area B.

Using map evidence, suggest **three** reasons for this.   **3**

Reference Diagram Q1B: A Hydro-electric Power Scheme

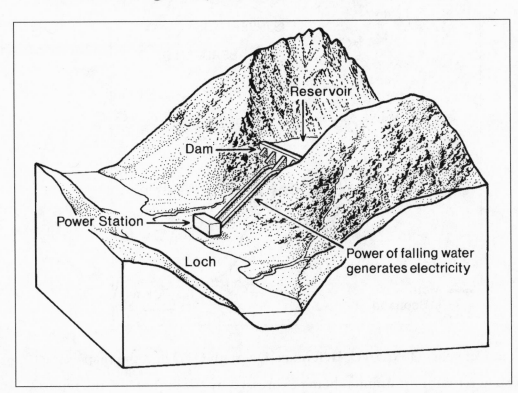

(*c*) Look at Reference Diagram Q1B.

There is a plan to construct a similar dam and power station in grid square 8853.

Using map evidence, describe the advantages **and** disadvantages of building such a scheme at this site.   **6**

Mark

KU

1. (continued)

Reference Text Q1C: Report of Economic Survey

"Torridon is an ideal place for a large scale tourist development. The benefits to the area would outweigh the disadvantages."

Reference Diagram Q1D: The Location of Torridon

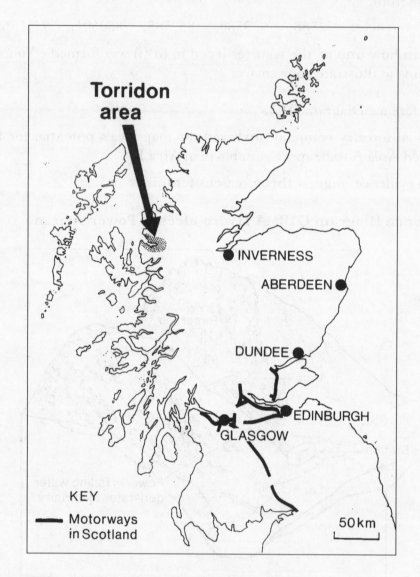

(*d*) Look at Reference Text Q1C, Reference Diagram Q1D and the map extract.

Do you agree with the opinion being expressed by the authors of the report?

Making reference to map evidence, give reasons for your answer.

1. (continued)

Reference Diagram Q1E: Field Sketch looking North to Ben Alligin from GR 862543

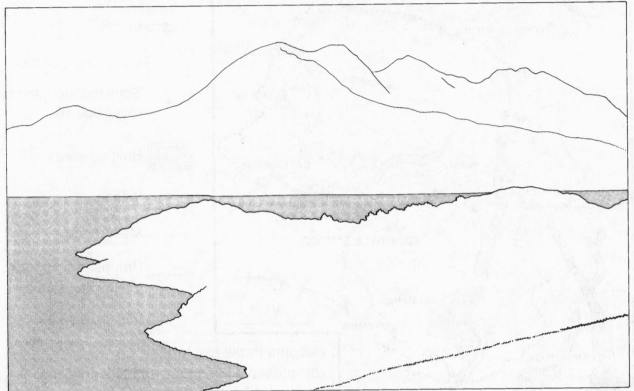

Marks

KU	ES

(e) A student has gathered information for a physical landscape investigation.

The information includes the outline field sketch shown above in Reference Diagram Q1E, a photograph of the same view, a geology map and the OS map extract.

What techniques should the student now use to **process** this information?

Justify your choices.

4

[Turn over

2.   **Reference Diagram Q2A: Loch Lomond and the Trossachs**

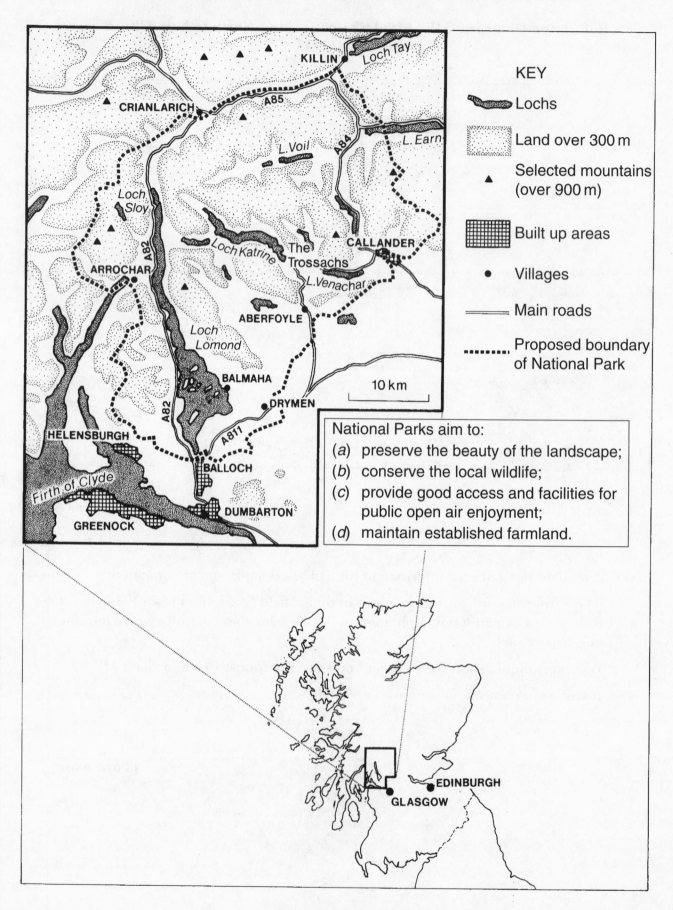

KEY

Lochs

Land over 300 m

Selected mountains (over 900 m)

Built up areas

Villages

Main roads

Proposed boundary of National Park

10 km

National Parks aim to:
(a) preserve the beauty of the landscape;
(b) conserve the local wildlife;
(c) provide good access and facilities for public open air enjoyment;
(d) maintain established farmland.

2. (continued)

Reference Diagram Q2B: Land Users in the Loch Lomond and Trossachs Area

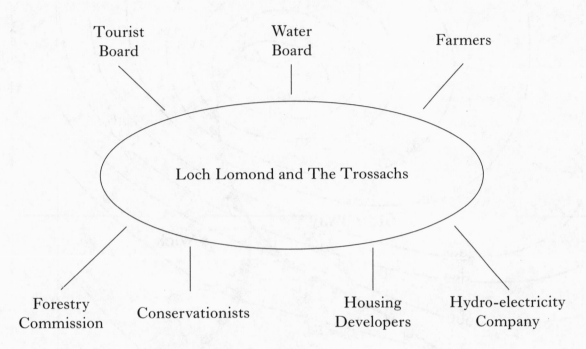

Study Reference Diagrams Q2A and Q2B.

Loch Lomond and The Trossachs was chosen as Scotland's first National Park.

Do you think all land users in Reference Diagram Q2B will welcome the establishment of this National Park?

Explain your answer.

6

[Turn over

3.

**Reference Diagram Q3: Synoptic Chart for British Isles
at 0700 hours on 31 August**

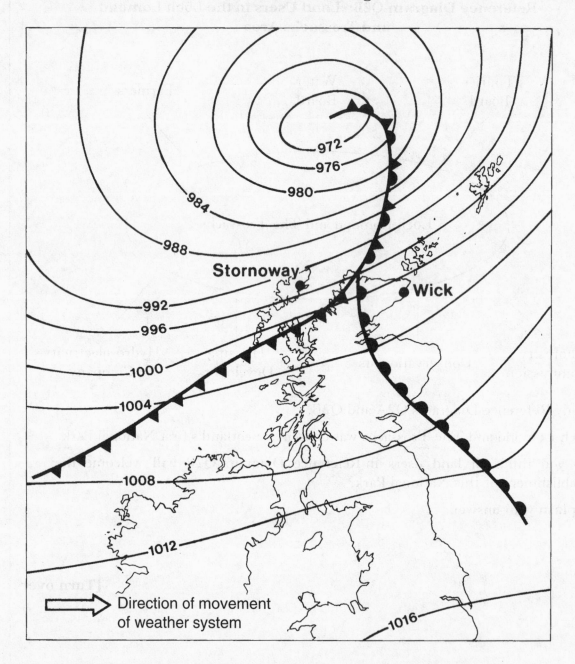

Direction of movement
of weather system

Look at Reference Diagram Q3.

A yacht race from Wick to Stornoway was due to start from Wick harbour at 8.00 am on 31 August.

At 7.00 am the Meteorological (Met) Office advised the race organisers to cancel the race.

With reference to the synoptic chart, **explain** why this advice was given.

5

4. Reference Diagram Q4A: Urban Transect along Queen's Road, Aberdeen

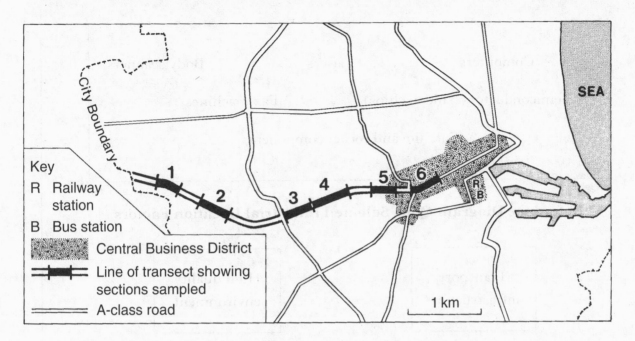

Reference Diagram Q4B: Data collected along Transect

Sample point	1	2	3	4	5	6
Building height (storeys)	2	2	3	4	4	4
Number of Pedestrians	2	4	7	8	17	64

Land use

Residential   Hotels   Public Buildings   Shops

Open space   Offices   Entertainment

Marks

KU   ES

Look at Reference Diagrams Q4A and Q4B.

(*a*) What techniques could have been used to gather the information in Reference Diagram Q4B?

Give reasons for your choices.

6

(*b*) **Explain** the changes that occur along the transect from the edge of the city to the centre.

6

Mark

KU

5.   **Reference Diagram Q5A: Examples of High-Technology Industry**

> Computers   Lasers   Body scanners
>
> Semiconductors (silicon chips)   Fax machines
>
> Satellite and rocket components

Reference Diagram Q5B: Selected Industrial Location Factors

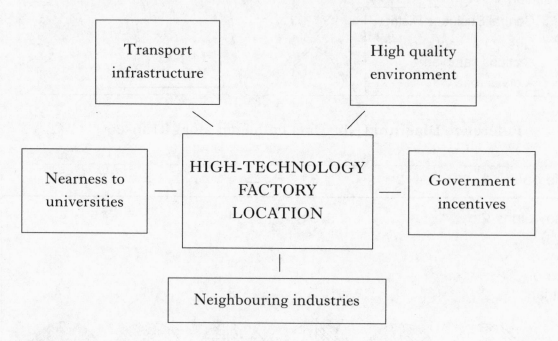

Study Reference Diagrams Q5A and Q5B.

Explain in what ways the factors listed above are important in the location of high-technology industries.

5

6.   **Reference Diagram Q6: Births per Woman and Infant Mortality
in Selected Countries**

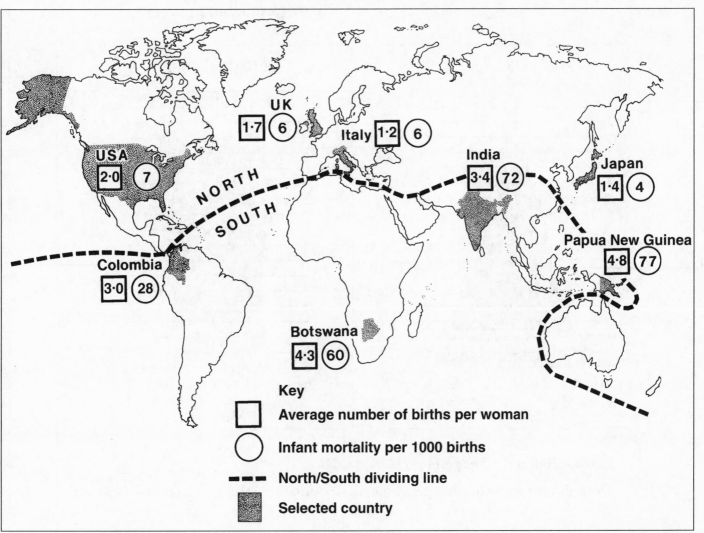

Key

☐ **Average number of births per woman**

◯ **Infant mortality per 1000 births**

– – – **North/South dividing line**

▨ **Selected country**

Marks

	KU	ES

(*a*) Look at Reference Diagram Q6.

Describe the patterns of births per woman and infant mortality, as shown in
Reference Diagram Q6.   **4**

(*b*) Explain the differences in the patterns between North and South.   **3**

(*c*) What measures have **developing** nations taken to reduce population growth
and infant mortality rates?   **4**

[Turn over

7.　　　**Reference Diagram Q7A:**　　　　　**Reference Diagram Q7B:**
　　Japan's Population Pyramid 1950　　**Japan's Population Pyramid 2050**
　　　　　　　　　　　　　　　　　　　　　　(projected figures)

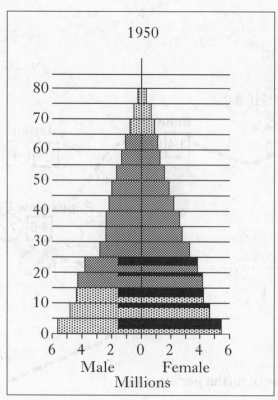

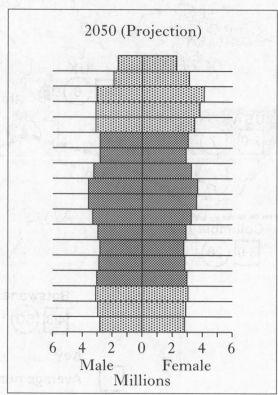

(a) Look at Reference Diagrams Q7A and Q7B.

Describe in detail the changes in Japan's population structure between 1950 and 2050.

(b) Do you agree that the changes in population structure will cause problems for the Japanese government by 2050?

State yes **or** no, and give reasons for your answer.

8. **Reference Table Q8A: Kenya—Exports and Imports**

Exports	%	Imports	%
Foodstuffs	59	Manufactured goods	40
Minerals and fuels	21	Minerals and fuels	23
Machinery and transport	9	Machinery and transport	13
Chemicals	4	Chemicals	11
Manufactured goods	3	Foodstuffs	9
Others	4	Others	4
Total ($ million)	$1028	Total ($ million)	$2136

Reference Table Q8B: Kenya—Direction of Trade

Trading Partners	% of Exports	% of Imports
European Union	43	43
(including UK)	(16)	(16)
African countries	18	2
United Arab Emirates	—	12
Japan	3	12
USA	4	4
Others	32	27

(a) Look at Reference Tables Q8A and Q8B.

Describe the pattern of Kenya's trade.

4

(b) Describe methods you could use to process the information shown in Reference Tables Q8A and Q8B.

Justify your choices.

6

[END OF QUESTION PAPER]

[BLANK PAGE]